Prayer with Searchers and Saints

Prayer with Searchers and Saints

by Edward Francis Gabriele

Saint Mary's Press
Christian Brothers Publications
Winona, Minnesota

Genuine recycled paper with 10% post-consumer waste.
Printed with soy-based ink.

The publishing team included Carl Koch, development editor; Jacqueline
M. Captain, copy editor; Barbara Bartelson, production editor and typeset-
ter; Maurine R. Twait, art director; Michael O. McGrath, cover designer
and illustrator; pre-press, printing, and binding by the graphics division of
Saint Mary's Press.

The acknowledgments continue on page 182.

Printed in the United States of America

Printing: 9 8 7 6 5 4 3 2 1

Year: 2006 05 04 03 02 01 00 99 98

ISBN 0-88489-526-2

Dedicated to the people of
Christ the Servant Lutheran Community
in Gaithersburg, Maryland . . .
women and men of faith,
radiating a this-worldly holiness
in their utterly human and humane lives;
always ready to wrestle with the meaning of the Gospel
for the sake of Christ's justice and peace,
and for the freedom and dignity
of all God's children without distinction.

Contents

The Lord's Prayer:
An Adaptation

Abba in heaven,
your name is holy!
Your justice come,
your will be done,
on earth as in the heavens.
Fill us this day
with all that we need.
Teach us to heal
as you have healed us.
Bring us not to the test,
but deliver us always
from the power of evil.
You alone are God.
And all belongs to you!

Preface

For each of us, the idea of holiness is an evolving reality. From the time we were young, we were presented with a multitude of images and lessons designed to inspire us to understand precisely what holiness and saintliness mean. Like other aspects of our Christian lives, the notions of saintliness and holiness are not static. They are dynamic realities that change as we grow and develop our humanness.

This volume of prayers, meditations, poetic compositions, and spiritual reflections attempts to expand our image of holiness and sainthood. These forty prayer services for individual or communal use celebrate the life, work, and Christian witness of a broad spectrum of individuals either canonically acknowledged as saints or whose quality of discipleship in Christ recommends them as heroic models for the Christian and world communities.

Over time I have come to appreciate that the saints of my life are largely unsung heroes who will most likely never be raised to official canonization. This constitutes a dramatic change from what I had believed at a young age. As a child I was more impressed by the celebrations of the saints than I was by the underlying strength of their authentic Christian holiness. Today I have come to appreciate that the essential mark of saintliness is humanness. The early church teaches us that the glory of God is the human being fully alive. I have come to appreciate the fullness of God in the human fullness that many individuals who cross my path portray. Just as the Scriptures themselves celebrate God's enduring word in human language that is awkward, impolite, coarse, and out of the ordinary, authentic holiness of life has entered my life as a gift from human beings whose lives would not necessarily be judged as the most religious or polite. Just as Francis of Assisi, a special patron in my life, was challenged by God to see the divine presence in a leper, God always stretches our mind and heart to see the activity of heaven in places that are surprising and sometimes humiliating to our human, and sometimes smug, sensibilities.

This work celebrates many types of saints with a general respect for the reformed liturgies of morning and evening prayer from the liturgy of the hours in the Roman tradition. The prayers can be used as valuable resources for individuals and communities seeking new ways of formulating prayer and new means of honoring those whose lives have borne a particular witness to Jesus. Regardless of how this book finally is employed, the prayers in it are simply more statements among millions of others that affirm how important it is to struggle with our ideas of the holy and how the divine presence is immersed in our world.

The presence of an untold number of persons and experiences is written between the lines of these pages. First of all, this volume owes its inspiration to the Rev. Harold H. Kerr, OPraem, the homilist whose work is cited in the introduction. Harry was my former high school guidance counselor, my Norbertine novice master at Daylesford Abbey, and an incredibly important friend in my journey of faith. His death in 1973 left a particular void in my life that was filled by the ever growing memory of his belief in me, especially when I most did not believe in myself.

Behind this work also stands the figure of my first abbot at Daylesford, the Rt. Rev. John Edward Neitzel. I remember with some humor how he always taught us that virtue stands in the middle of things. If he were to take that definition to an absurd conclusion, then his own service of the Gospel could hardly then ever be judged as virtuous! For his service of the Gospel was a passion, a "fire in his belly" as he put it, hardly "in the middle" or reasonably balanced. John's consistent encouragement for my theological writing and teaching has been an important gift to me, especially when God's closing of one door was not automatically followed by the opening of another.

I also need to call attention to those to whom this volume is dedicated. In 1995, through a happy accident of needing resource material for another publication, I became acquainted with the Rev. Peter Bastien and the members of Christ the Servant Lutheran Community (CTS). That first meeting developed into consultation and guest lecture work for about a year. Today I am privileged to serve this community of truly Christian women and men as ecumenical theologian-in-residence. The humanity and profound holiness of the CTS family of faith is an astounding gift of grace. The men and women are so passionately in love with their Christ that they can do nothing but love one another and bear the gifts of justice and peace to all who suffer.

Finally, I must thank those whose editorial assistance made this work possible. Petty Officer Yusef Miller of the African American Heritage Committee at the Naval Medical Research Institute in Bethesda, Maryland, provided background materials on Sojourner Truth. Calvin Chue, Daniel Winfield, and Lieutenant Malcolm Johns were instrumental in the acquiring of essential materials through their personal instruction in the use of Internet resources. Carl Koch and Saint Mary's Press generously provided many of the other resource materials for the histories and works of the various persons represented and celebrated in this volume. Furthermore, it was Carl Koch himself who first initiated the concept for this volume, encouraged it, refined it, reshaped my awkward constructions, and brought it finally to the table of faith. Of particular significance, Carl provided new insights and configurations to the text. In a particularly vital manner, Carl's critical editing and masterful crafting made this text increasingly richer for those who will benefit from its publication. As in other projects with Saint Mary's, I am deeply in Carl's debt for his kind regard of the theological reflection and publication gifts that God has given to me.

In a word, a true saint is one who has the courage to be human. The liturgy and our faith center on the fundamental belief that "The Word became flesh." If we would celebrate the saints, and thereby celebrate ourselves as God's holy ones as well, we need not look to legend and marble figures. We need only look into the mirror. In finding ourselves, we find the saints. In seeing ourselves precisely as we are in our sinfulness, we see holiness. In loving ourselves, we love the eternal God who loves us and chooses to live within our human flesh and blood.

Introduction

Reflections on Celebrating Saints

A number of years ago, my then-novice master, Fr. Harry Kerr, recounted in a homily a story that reveals the nature of the saints.

> A mother went into a church on a quiet afternoon with her young son. From a busy day, she took time for prayer and reflection. Entering into a church building for the first time, the young boy was amazed by many things, but especially by the traditional stained-glass windows. He tugged on his mother's coat and asked her what they were. Almost without thinking, the mother told her boy that those were saints. A moment passed. His mother's words percolated. He interrupted his mother's return to prayer by tugging on her coat again. "Mom! Mom!" His mother answered with some irritation, "What?" The young boy then exclaimed with one of those whispers that could be heard in the rafters: "I know what saints are! They let the light come in."

Out of the mouths of babes. . . .

The practice of venerating the saints is as old as the church itself. Beginning with the respect given to the memory of the first disciples, the mother of Jesus, and the honoring of the martyrs during various persecutions in the Greco-Roman world, the place of the *sancti* in the church was given special prayerful remembrance by individuals and in the community's worship. In later centuries, due to numerous substantiated abuses, veneration of the saints came under sharp criticism and even repudiation in Reformation communities. The veneration of the saints, like all other aspects of Christian life and spirituality, did need and will always need to be reformulated and revised. Nevertheless, the tradition of praying for and with exemplars of our faith remains a vital part of the experience of Christian prayer.

If we believe that Jesus is the sole mediator of salvation and that Jesus himself intercedes for us with God, what then is the place of the saints? Who are they? Why do we pray for and with them? How should one approach this ancient practice of prayer?

Who Are the Saints?

For many people, a saint is someone who has been declared a saint either through popular acclaim as in the cases of martyrs and leaders of the early Christian communities or through the canonization processes established much later in the church. On the other hand, the spirit of the Protestant Reformation invites us to look to the Scriptures, where we are told that the church is the community of God's holy ones, the saints. The answer to who is a saint may lie somewhere in between these two interpretations.

The early church proclaimed that the glory of God is the human being fully alive. The saints are heroic because their lives demonstrate that they are fully grounded in their own humanness. The saints are complete human beings endowed with many of the same tasks of maturity, the same successes, the same aspirations, and the same defects and problems that we all face. From the Apostle Peter to Thérèse of Lisieux, all the saints confront the forces of the human shadow. Real saints are grounded thoroughly in their humanness.

Saints are also grounded completely in Jesus Christ, in the quest for God's light in their lives and in the world. Sanctity is not simply measured in making contributions to social progress. Sanctity requires the conversion of one's life into the person of Jesus Christ, crucified and risen. Saints are men and women who engage in the joys and intense struggles of prayer and conversion of life—hardly an easy path. Even the great mystic Teresa of Ávila confessed that her consolations and ecstasies were only occasional. Like the rest of us, the saints know well the experience of the desert, of depression, of feeling abandoned. Of course, Jesus suf-fered these experiences as well. The mark of the saint is fidelity to the process of becoming a new person in Jesus. Wherever the human spirit tenaciously clings to the gift of faith in Jesus, there sanctity is found.

Saints embrace the world. After all, Jesus took on our human flesh. He walked among us, healed sick peo-ple, preached the good news that God loves human beings, and ate with anyone who would share a meal with him. Real saints serve in the world with the same tenacious love with which the Word became our flesh.

Clearly the saints have served the world in various ways. Hidden away, hermits, nuns, and monks witness to the power of prayer and solitude. Like Jesus in the desert, their quiet presence reminds us that all activity for good can be sustained only if it is rooted in attentive love, sustained hope, strong faith renewed through med-itation. Other saints take to the streets to care for or-phans, struggle against injustice, bind up the wounds of a battered world. Saints witness to the presence of a God who created the world, who loves the world, who gives us the world to steward, and who embraces our worldly lives with passion and delight.

Why Venerate the Saints?

The human animal is a communal creature. The biblical story of Creation captures a truth about the nature of being human: we are not meant to be alone. Social psy-chologists remind us that our experience of ourselves is the experience of incompletion. The ancient Greeks captured our need to merge with other people in their term *eros*. In its origins *eros* does not necessarily imply sexual activity. It is the energy within us that realizes the void within the soul and moves us out of ourselves in search of those others who may bring us to peace and completion. The fundamental truth about our human nature is its radical contingency and interdependence on others.

Jesus' experience of Judaism was not an individualis-tic one. His disciples were bonded by his presence into a community of faith. The Resurrection makes clear that

Christianity is not an individual experience either. Baptism into Christ is baptism into a communal experience. Paul confronted this fact on the road to Damascus. He thought that he was stamping out a heretical sect. He discovered that those he was persecuting were a community who by their very nature were the presence of the Messiah. To be born again into Christ is to be born into a community of faith, and this community is one that transcends both time and space. As baptized members of the Body of Christ, we are connected not only to this world, but also to all those who have gone before us marked with the sign of faith.

Just as our families venerate in story, memorials, objects, and rituals the memory of our loved ones who have died, the Christian family remembers the contributions of those who have paved the path of faith before us. While the ways we venerate our Christian ancestors differ in each culture, believers of every age appreciate the impact and contribution that the saints have made and will continue to make. Our veneration of the holy ones, our belief in the communion of saints, the great cloud of witnesses, is an acceptance of our communitarian nature and our belief that we are the Body of Christ, God's holy people in every age and in every place.

Venerating the Saints Authentically

The church has never worshiped the saints. In fact, considerable effort was made in past ages to differentiate between the worship we give to God alone and the veneration we give to our saintly sisters and brothers. Marks of honor given to the saints have been judged as worship. In some cultures and times, veneration of the saints actually bordered on worship. The church, however, has never endorsed the worship of the saints: venerate, meaning to regard with respect and admiration, yes; worship, meaning to reverence as a divine being, no.

In the liturgy and in private prayer, many Christians pray to the saints. This may seem strange to some, and rightly so. But praying to saints may be better understood when we think about how often we ask our friends and relatives to pray for us. The saints, our partners in the Body of Christ, are our friends, too. We are collectively the *amici in Christum*, friends in Christ's love. We ask their prayers and love as we would ask for the remembrance and love of a parent, a sibling, a friend, a colleague, or a member of our community. We need their intercession as much as we need the intercession of our friends in this world. We need their prayers not to change the mind of God but to ask for the strength of the Spirit so that we can remain faithful to the Gospel despite what adventures may come our way in this life.

We best venerate the saints, honor their memory, and cherish their witness when we ask them to be beside us in prayer and in service. Thus, the Orthodox place sacred icons around their worship areas. Through icons they express their belief that the communion of saints is gathered as the community prays. The saints abide with us. And we abide with the saints in the one act of giving glory to God.

We venerate the saints when we pray with them in the context of the Scriptures and the church's prayer, when we reverence the humanness of our Christian faith, when we remember that our lives are a celebration of our living relationship with Jesus, and when we realize that our prayers with the saints send us into the world for the service of others and all creation. Authentic veneration of the saints can never be an escape from the world. Quite the opposite. Venerating the saints inevitably must give us the strength to engage the world, to bear the message of Jesus into the world.

Conclusion

As the young boy announced in the story cited at the beginning of this introduction, saints are truly those who "let the light in." Like the refraction of light into the colors of the rainbow, the thousands upon thousands of members of the cloud of witnesses reflect in unlimited human portraits the many ways the grace of Jesus takes flesh in the world. The saints remind us that light itself is the presence of Jesus. They remind us that the light of Christ must shine on and through anyone who wishes to be a disciple of Jesus. They remind us that the light of Christ flames forth not for ourselves alone but for others, for all creation, for history.

Each Christmas we celebrate that the Word became flesh. The liturgies of Christmas remind us that a great light has come to Earth. Heaven has wedded Earth in a marvelous exchange. Such glory demands witnesses. The Word must become flesh in our flesh. The light of heaven must illumine the heart, mind, and body. The marriage of heaven is with our earth, the earth of our history and our condition with all its promises and all its tragedies.

To celebrate the saints is to celebrate ourselves. To ask for their companionship and prayerful remembrance is to be reminded that we are called to be prayerful companions and servants of one another as well. To serve in the path of holiness is to be sent into the world to laugh with those who laugh, to mourn with those who mourn, to hunger and thirst with those whose belly and heart crave for the touch of love and the food of justice.

Praying with the searchers and saints of all time is not merely an act of piety superfluous to the message of the Gospel. It is the natural overflow of our belief in Jesus who entered fully into our human community as the presence of God that we might celebrate our human community and all of creation as the place where God has freely chosen in love to dwell.

Ruth and Naomi
Builders of Communities
of Friendship and Faith

God created us to be in relationship. We are creatures of community. However, intimacy demands openness of heart and soul, and it requires sacrifices. The story of Ruth and Naomi's faithful friendship shows the power of mutual care born out of personal loss and tragedy. After their suffering, Naomi could leave Ruth free to choose her own path, but Ruth chooses to remain and journey with her mother-in-law and friend. From the ground of their friendship, Ruth—the outsider, the Gentile—is drawn to the people and God of Israel and is listed among the the ancestors of David and Jesus.

MORNING

As we rise to the splendor of this new day, we celebrate with all the saints the cords of God's love that bind us together as one family of faith. Called to journey with one another on the pathways to God's Reign, we pray with Ruth and Naomi that we may be drawn to love one another and that this love will give us strength for the tasks of discipleship in Christ.

Call to Prayer

God, fountain of love,
you are the wellspring from which
our human thirst for love is quenched.
We praise and adore you for the gift of your loving
that has been given to us in Christ
and that is the cornerstone of every community.
With Ruth, Naomi, and all your friends,
we rejoice this day for the presence of the Spirit

Praise

who binds us as one family of faith,
proclaiming your message of mercy and justice.
With all the saints, we celebrate the gift of salvation
that is the hope of all those
who long for the touch of human love.

Reading

Ruth sobbed at Naomi's feet and begged her not
to send her away. She said:
"Wherever you go, I will go.
Wherever you stay, I will stay.
Your people will be my people.
Your God will be my God."
Naomi then realized the devotion of her daughter-
in-law and friend. Together they remained and
walked the pathways of their faith in God and with
one another. (Ruth 1:15–18)

Acclamations

On this new day of grace, God joins us together that we
might strengthen one another in love for the journey of
faith in Christ. In joy we pray: *Honor, love, and praise be
yours!*

- We adore you, God, who is the fountain of human
  friendship and the wellspring of human love, as we
  pray . . .
- We are filled with gratitude for the gift of friends and
  loved ones in our life, as we pray . . .
- We worship you, God, who gives us in Ruth and Naomi the image of faith-filled companions in grace, as
  we pray . . .
- We are filled with joy for the blessing of friendship
  that sustains us in joy and lessens our pain in times of
  sorrow, as we pray . . .

Closing

Faithful God, even when we wander from your friendship, you remain with us in unbroken and unshakable
love. In the Resurrection of Christ, you sealed your love
for us for all time. In the journey of Ruth and Naomi,
you give us a living example of the blessing of human
love and friendship. Teach us by your Holy Spirit never
to abandon the friends you give us in life until that day

when you gather all peoples into the one community of your loving. We ask this as all things through Jesus our Messiah forever and ever. Amen.

As the hours of daylight grow short, we give God thanks for the blessing of friends and loved ones who grace our home and life with joy. We pray this night in a particular way for those who are oppressed. In the power of their solidarity with one another, they keep alive the light of liberty for all those searching for the blessings of peace and concord.

Call to Prayer

God of all loving,
through the presence of Jesus among us
you keep alive the flames of freedom
that call our human family to the glory of friendship
with you and with one another.
This night we give you praise and thanks
as we confess the diverse ways
our selfishness has torn asunder
the bonds of human communion.
The gift of friendship shared by Naomi and Ruth
stands before us as a beacon of light,
beckoning us to build for you in the Spirit
a family of faith-filled friends
whose loyalty and love are signs of hope
for all those who struggle in oppression.
With the saints of every time and place
we celebrate the light of hope
that moves us to build for you a communion of hearts
in which the forces of bondage and fear have no power.

Thanksgiving

As one who is a prisoner for love's sake, I beg you to be united with one another. Put aside all differences. Deal with each other in love, caring and patience. May your unity be based on the unity of faith. For there is one Christ, one faith, one baptism, and one God who binds us together as the foundation of hope. (Ephesians 4:1–6)

Reading

Intercessions

We know that the spirit of God can take away all that divides us and can place into our midst the gift of faithful friendship. We offer the needs of our hopeful heart, as we pray: *Keep us mindful of your love.*

- For the church, that our care and concern for one another may be a sign of hope for all people, let us pray . . .
- For the human heart searching for love, that the Spirit may open us to offer and receive the gift of friendship, let us pray . . .
- For all those who live in sorrow and loneliness, that God may send friends into their life with whom they can share the joy of Christ's presence, let us pray . . .
- For the sick and the suffering, that the friendships we share may make us generous for their service, let us pray . . .

Closing

Repeat morning's closing.

Mary
Mother of Jesus

Mary, a young woman without stature in her culture and time, said yes to a heavenly visitor and signaled the beginning of our redemption in Christ. Because she unconditionally accepted God's invitation despite her questions, Mary is the singular model for what it means to be a faithful disciple of Christ: open to God's word, human enough to question and wrestle with God's will, graced enough to surrender and trust.

Call to Prayer

At the beginning of this day, we remember the life and witness of Mary, the mother of Jesus, who gave flesh to the incarnate Word of God in her heart and in her womb. Called like Mary to give flesh to the presence of Christ in our life, we pray that we may be faithful witnesses of the gift of salvation in our every word and deed.

Praise

Be praised above the heavens,
O gracious God,
for the dawning of your sun of justice
upon a people who walked in darkness.
Each day we set our face
toward the fullness of your peace.
We rejoice for the memory and witness
of the Mother whom you consecrated
from the first moment of her life
to give birth to the Word
as the dawn of our salvation.

The Mother of Jesus
is the image of your church
and the leaven of our discipleship.
She who bore the Promise of the Ages
is the living reminder
that all who profess Jesus as the Christ
must bring to birth the Gospel
to all the nations of the earth for all time.

Reading

Before all else was created, God fashioned the gift of wisdom in love. Before all eternity, God created wisdom and loved it. No one can ever know the roots of wisdom for they are found only in the mind of God. God alone is wise. God took wisdom and poured it out upon all the earth. God took wisdom and made it a gift to all the living. (Sirach 1:4–10)

Acclamations

With Mary and all the saints, we praise the God of love as we pray: *Honor, love, and praise be yours!*
- We worship you, God, who brings peace to all the nations, as we pray . . .
- We glorify your name, Holy One, who has called us to bear witness to the peace of heaven's joys, as we pray . . .
- We raise our voice to honor you, immortal God, who gives to us Christ as our Savior, as we pray . . .
- We are filled with wonder for your mercy, God of sun and moon, as we pray . . .

Closing

God of all salvation, we give you thanks this day for Mary, the exemplar of your church. Fill us with the grace of the Holy Spirit that, like Mary, we might be faithful messengers of the Gospel of life. We ask this as all things through Jesus our Messiah forever and ever. Amen.

Call to Prayer

As evening falls, we gather like the early disciples eager for the presence of Christ who leads us always on toward endless day. As in the upper room, Mary is in our midst as our companion in the faith. In the light of her example, we are encouraged to be faithful to our common call to be disciples of Jesus.

Thanksgiving

All thanks be to you,
O God of all mercy,
for the gifts that you have bestowed upon us
in Jesus, the light of the world.
As evening's shades descend upon the earth,
we beg for the gift of your eternal brilliance
that enlightened the life of Mary.
In her life, she proclaimed the new justice
found only in Christ Jesus.
In your salvation,
the rich go hungry
while the poor have their fill;
the proud are humbled to the dust
while the lowly are raised to heights never dreamed.

Reading

So many things of wonder had come to pass. A strange visitor. And stranger questions still. In the end, a "yes." Now a path of service to her kinswoman so lately come to mothering. From the mouth of her kin, again strange words fell upon her ears. Things Mary never would have dreamed. Things her world had forbidden her to hear. And yet she heard them. And in her heart there was no fear. Only words of ecstasy and praise echoing the song of her forebears: "Every fiber of my being magnifies the goodness of God!" (Luke 2:39–47)

Intercessions

God has brought us in Christ to a new birth and has washed us clean from all fear. As a holy people, let us present to God our needs as we pray: *Keep us mindful of your love.*

- For all who acknowledge Jesus as Savior, that the spirit of God might move us to bear the Word to every nation, let us pray . . .
- For all the nations, that the image of Mary as the faithful disciple might be a leaven of peace and justice, let us pray . . .
- For our community, that the example of Mary might move us to seek the gift of strength in our service of all God's people, let us pray . . .
- For those sick and suffering people, that Mary, as friend and comforter, may call on her Son to send healing and rest, let us pray . . .

Closing   Repeat morning's closing.

Joseph
Husband of Mary

Only briefly present in the scriptural stories about Jesus, Joseph has endured as one of the most popular saints in Christian history. Called beyond the expectations and norms of his age, the husband of Mary possessed courageous trust. Joseph stood loyally and unwaveringly as husband in the first household of faith. He also provides a model of simple greatness as a worker-saint. Because of his courage and steadfastness to God's will, Joseph is rightly the patron of the entire church community.

MORNING

Call to Prayer

As this day begins, we call to mind Joseph, husband of Mary, whose witness to salvation's dawn was filled with the courage of the Holy Spirit. Like Joseph, God stretches our mind and heart and calls us to the Gospel of life that is beyond all logic and reasoning.

Praise

Blessed may you be,
O God of Israel and ancient of days!
At the dawn of salvation
you called a Chosen People
to give witness to your law
that delights every human heart
in search of truth and justice and love.
You raised up David, your servant,
and established from him
a royal priesthood to offer you praise and adoration.
From the line of David, you called Joseph of Nazareth
to be the husband of Mary,
the guardian of Jesus,

and husband in the first household of faith.
As you called Joseph,
so too do you call your holy people in every age
to establish human communion,
to fashion works and words of praise and love,
and thus build up our world
as one family to thirst for your peace.

Reading

From the depths of my heart, I will sing forever of all
that you have done for us, O loving God. You are
faithful in every generation. It is your steadfast love
that has raised us up. You have made a Covenant
with David, your chosen one. You established David's
line for all ages to give you praise and thanks before
every nation and family. You have established us
forever to always sing of your goodness and to announce your peace to every generation. (Psalm
89:1–4)

Acclamations

With Joseph and with every saint, we praise the God of
love as we pray: *Honor, love, and praise be yours!*
- We worship you, God, who calls our world to be one
  family of love, as we pray . . .

- We adore you, God, who has established every family to give witness to the unbounding depth of love to all the world, as we pray . . .
- We lift our voice to praise you, God, whose gifts of justice and peace are the foundation for our life, as we pray . . .
- We are filled with wonder for your mercy, Creator of sun and moon, as we pray . . .

Closing

Loving and gracious God, you raised up Joseph to be the husband of Mary, the guardian of Jesus, and part of your first household of faith. Silently witnessing to your justice, he was faithful to the law. Through your Spirit, teach us to imitate his example and proclaim your justice in our every word and deed. We ask this as all things through Jesus our Messiah forever and ever. Amen.

EVENING

Call to Prayer

As the darkness falls around us, we gather in our homes, grateful for the blessings that God has bestowed upon us. In our mind and heart, we remember the witness to the word that was at the heart of Joseph's life. We ask that his example may root our own faith in a deeper trust of God's will.

Thanksgiving

All praise and thanks be yours,
O God of Israel and all the world.
In the nighttime of our life,
you move in our midst
and protect us under the shadow of your wings.
In our dreaming and our waking,
you reveal your loving plan to us
and ask us always to announce your gift of peace.
As with holy Joseph,
you call us to tend your household of faith
and keep your lamp of justice burning brightly
for all those who fear the shadow of death.

Reading

I stirred in my sleep, uncomfortable because of the news I had received today. The law bids me to one course of action; my heart, to another. And now this voice in my dreaming tells me: "Fear not. This child will be the Holy One." How can I do otherwise than open my heart and home? The God of our ancestors is always in the realm of the strange and the awe-filled. I pray, O God, help me to trust more deeply. Let your trust be pitched within my heart, that your Emmanuel may pitch your tent again in our midst! (Matthew 1:18–25)

Intercessions

In every age, God raises up those whose lives of faith inspire our own. With Joseph and all the saints we present our needs before God, as we pray: *Keep us mindful of your love.*

- For Christians throughout the world, that we may imitate Joseph's fidelity, courage, and trust, let us pray . . .
- For every human family, that in the example of Joseph we may allow the Holy Spirit to build us into households of faith, let us pray . . .
- For those whose faith has been weakened by tragedy and fear, that the power of the Holy Spirit may bring them consolation and peace, let us pray . . .
- For all those who are victims of injustice, hatred, bigotry, and prejudice, that the Holy Spirit may inspire us to deeds of justice and freedom on their behalf, let us pray . . .

Closing

Repeat morning's closing.

John the Baptizer
Herald of the Messiah,
Martyr for Truth

*The Gospel writers portray Jesus as saying that none born
of woman could be greater than John the Baptizer. John's
prophetic message was highly volatile, calling for the immedi-
ate reform of the life of individuals and ancient Israel itself.
John's own life was imbued with the demands of a rigorous
and fiery spirituality. Like others who preached the truth with
such zeal, he lost his life at the hands of his enemies. His
abiding legacy compels believers to make straight the way
of the Messiah in one's body, mind, spirit, and manner of
living. John also challenges us to zeal, fire in the soul, and
strength of action for the work of God's Reign.*

MORNING

As the morning dew gathers on the grasses, we hear in
our life the voice of one crying out from the desert:
"Prepare the way of the Lord. Make straight the pathways of your life to Christ." The message of the Baptizer
continues to be heard in our time, and we ask the Spirit
to give us the courage to follow in his path of reform and
conversion.

Call to Prayer

God of sages and prophets,
your word is life itself.
To prepare the way of salvation,
you raised up John the Baptizer
as the prophet of the Messiah,
making straight our pathways to Jesus.
This day we give you praise and adoration
for the voice of the Baptizer that calls out to us still

Praise

31

and bids us to open our heart to the fire of the Spirit
who burns up our sinful chaff
and then molds our heart as a fitting vessel of grace.
Your Spirit moves within us this day,
inviting us to ready ourselves at every daybreak
for the coming of Christ's grace again into our flesh.

Reading

Elijah appeared in our life wrapped with fire from
heaven.
He shut the heavens and burned up the sacrifices to
false gods in our midst.
No prophet is as glorious as Elijah
who was taken from our midst in a chariot of flame
up to the heavens.
We wait for his return hopeful that he will lead the
heart of children back toward their parents in
love.
When Elijah comes again,
Israel shall be established forever.
(Sirach 48:1–4, 9–11)

Acclamations

The word of God is spirit and truth. This day we listen
for the word alive in the voices of prophets like John the
Baptizer. In joy we pray: *Honor, love, and praise be yours!*

- We adore you, God, whose living Word comes to the
  earth and accomplishes your holy will in fidelity, as
  we pray . . .
- We are filled with wonder for the prophets of our
  time who call us, like John the Baptizer, back to the
  pathways of faithful service, as we pray . . .
- We worship you, God, whose courage moved John
  the Baptizer to announce the truth even at the price
  of his own blood, as we pray . . .
- We are filled with joy at the presence of the Spirit
  among us who moves us to make straight all pathways
  to Jesus our Messiah, as we pray . . .

God of life, in the fullness of time you raised up John the Baptizer to be the final herald for the coming of the Messiah. John's voice rang out in the desert and called your people to repent their sins. Open our ears to hear his message once again. Empty us of everything that is not born of your love. And touch our flesh at least with the presence of your Word, who alone is the life for which our desert soul thirsts and yearns. We ask this as all things through Jesus our Messiah forever and ever. Amen.

Closing

EVENING

In this evening hour, the light of Christ is kindled in our midst, calling us from the slavery of sin to the brilliant freedom of grace. The light of Christ descends upon us and warms us to the gift of ongoing conversion. We pray this night for our conversion and the conversion of every heart into the truth and love of the Messiah.

Call to Prayer

All praise and thanks to you,
eternal God of life,
for the baptism of fire
that is kindled in our midst
at this evening hour.
The Baptizer is with us,
calling out,
opening our eyes anew
to the presence of your Lamb in our midst.
Fearful though our heart might be,
yet we are given the Spirit of courage
to proclaim in every evening and every dawning
the salvation that is ours in Christ,
which has marked the lintels of the world
and set us apart as a faithful, servant people.

Thanksgiving

John baptized at the river Jordan. One day his eyes caught the sight of the other. And John proclaimed: "Behold, the Lamb! The one who takes away the sins of the world." At first he had not recognized the other. So many crowds, so many hearts searching

Reading

and pleading for something of faith and life. But in the fateful meeting of their eyes, John saw. And then he knew that the other who caught his vision ranked ahead of him and was marked by the divine Spirit. And the baptizing prophet proclaimed again: "This is God's Chosen." (John 1:29–34)

Intercessions

We celebrate with John the Baptizer the presence of the lamb of God who takes away the sins of the world. Bearing the needs of the world, we are confident of the gift of salvation as we pray: *Keep us mindful of your love.*

- For the church, that we may find our rest and salvation in the living person of Jesus, let us pray . . .
- For the nations, that the Spirit may open their ears to the voice of the prophets calling for a conversion to justice, let us pray . . .
- For those whose heart and will are weak, that God will send to them prophets of consolation and peace, let us pray . . .
- For all those who are called to be prophetic voices in the world and in the church, that the Spirit may strengthen them when they suffer for the sake of the Word of life, let us pray . . .

Closing

Repeat morning's closing.

Martha, Mary, and Lazarus of Bethany
A Family of Faith

The Gospels portray Jesus as having a special friendship with Martha, Mary, and Lazarus of Bethany. In the Gospel of Luke, Jesus proclaims that Mary, sitting at his feet instead of helping her sister, Martha, with domestic work, is particularly blessed. Jesus is not showing a preference for contemplation over action. This scene actually shows Mary—a woman—daring to learn the Law at the feet of the Rabbi, something unthinkable in that age. In the Gospel of John, Jesus raises Lazarus from the dead as his sisters proclaim their faith. In both cases, Martha, Mary, and Lazarus provide us with fitting portraits displaying human families, whether traditional or emergent, that are brought to completion by being founded on faith in Christ. These stories also show the tender love that characterized Jesus' friendship with these three people.

MORNING

At this new day we celebrate that God has called us to be one family of faith, one communion of love in Christ. With Martha, Mary, and Lazarus, we pray that the Spirit will move us to learn always the meaning of Christ's one law of love.

Call to Prayer

O God, you are the solid foundation for families
and the center of human communion.
This day we praise and adore you
for the love that you have poured out on us
in the gift of salvation in Christ.

Praise

Christ is the teacher
who opens our mind and heart
to the unfolding vistas of your law.
Christ beckons us to sit before you,
to be immersed in your law,
and to prefer your love above all things.
With Martha, Mary, and Lazarus,
we celebrate your binding us in unity
and forming us to be a community of faithful witnesses
made fresh each day by grace
to announce your salvation to the whole world.

Reading

She sits at his feet, never thinking to help with the household chores. She sits there listening. A scandal. A woman daring to learn the Torah and to hear the word of life from the Rabbi. And then he, our friend, proclaims her blessed. Such strange things to hear and to behold. He makes all things new—and uncomfortable. (Luke 10:38–42)

Acclamations

At the start of this new day, God calls us again to hear the word of life that brings us joy and stretches our heart and mind. In joy we pray: *Honor, love, and praise be yours!*

- We adore you, God, who sent us the Messiah to be the solid center of all communities of faith, as we pray . . .
- We are filled with gratitude for the thirst within us that makes us yearn beyond all convention to know the love of Christ, as we pray . . .
- We worship you, God, who calls the church to be one communion, preaching one Gospel of life, as we pray . . .
- We are filled with joy for the companionship we have with Martha, Mary, Lazarus and all the friends of Christ, as we pray . . .

Closing

Center of the universe, you did not create us to be alone, but fashioned us to live in harmony with you and one another. In the image of Martha, Mary, and Lazarus of Bethany, you have given to your people a fitting example of holiness on which your church may build up the human family. Teach us like Mary to prefer your love above all else. Teach us like Martha to work for the service of Christ. Teach us like Lazarus to allow the power of Christ to raise us to new life. We ask this as all things through Jesus our Messiah forever and ever. Amen.

EVENING

Call to Prayer

As the evening hour draws us to thoughts of home, we call to mind those who experience desperate loneliness. Trusting like Martha, Mary, and Lazarus that Christ can raise all people to new life, let your Spirit move among us to welcome all those who yearn for love and affection into our family of faith and friendship.

Thanksgiving

Living God,
this night we give you praise and thanks
for the Risen Christ who is ever in our midst,
dispelling the power of death and darkness.
Through all the ages,
with Martha, Mary, and Lazarus of Bethany,
we proclaim the power of the Resurrection
and announce that death has no more sting.
You are the God who desires
full life for your beloved family on earth.
In Christ you raise us to the glory of life eternal
and hold out to us the bright promise of heaven
that human doubt cannot dim.
Your Spirit moves in our midst this night
that we might never despair,
but keep the fires of our faith burning
for the enlightenment of the whole human family.

Reading

When you look at me, do you see the Resurrection? When you look at me, do you see life? If you see me truly, do you know that you will never die? If you look at me from the depth of your heart and faith, do you know that you will live forever and that death has no more power? But do you? Do you really believe? (John 11:25–27)

Intercessions   We believe that Christ is the Resurrection and the life. Confident that God will always ground the human family on the rising of Jesus, we bear the needs of the world to the God of all life as we pray: *Keep us mindful of your love.*

- For the church, that we may be faithful to the proclamation of the death and the Resurrection of Christ for all time, let us pray . . .
- For every human family, that the power of Christ's Resurrection may be the center of their love, affection, and care for one another, let us pray . . .
- For homeless, sick, suffering, and indigent people, that they may know the blessings of Christ's rising in this life, let us pray . . .
- For the dead, that they may be embraced now in the Resurrection of Christ by Martha, Mary, Lazarus, and all the saints, let us pray . . .

Closing   Repeat morning's closing.

Peter, Paul, and the Apostles
Witnesses and Proclaimers of the Gospel

In our age, we appreciate that apostolic succession holds a far deeper religious reality than simply the laying on of hands from one church leader to another. Apostolic succession implies the fidelity of succeeding generations to the experience of the faith handed down from the first Apostles and disciples, a faith that is grounded in the living experience of the person of Jesus Christ, crucified and risen. It is important, then, that we honor the life and witness of Peter, Paul, and the first Apostles as those who, with the power of the Holy Spirit, began the sacred tradition of handing on the faith for the salvation of every generation in the history of the world.

MORNING

As this new day begins, we honor the life and memory of Peter, Paul, and the first witnesses and Apostles of Christ. God called these witnesses to be the first preachers of the Good News of Jesus. We pray this day that we might faithfully continue their ministry of spreading the Gospel.

Call to Prayer

Living foundation of all salvation,
this day we give you praise and adoration
for the gift of salvation that has come to us
in the death and Resurrection of Christ Jesus.
Christ is the mediator of all grace.
From the beginning, he called to himself
friends and companions in his service

Praise

39

who would be urged by the Holy Spirit
to proclaim the Good News to the ends of the earth.
As we honor the memory of Peter, Paul, and the first
    Apostles,
we celebrate with joy the faith that they have given to
    us,
a faith that the Spirit now urges us to proclaim
in thought, word, and service.
All praise to you, O God, for your unfolding salvation
that comes to us in Christ
and that is the life of the world.

Reading

"You are the Christ, the Son of the Living God."
The statement fell like a rock among them. The
silence was long. The unspeakable had been said.
And Jesus suddenly smiled with an almost impercep-
tible laughter in his next words. "Oh Peter, you must
be rock to have said such a thing. And for this part I
declare that it is on this kind of rock that my church
will be built: the rock of faith that goes beyond what
humans would expect to hear." (Matthew 16:16–18)

Acclamations

With Peter, Paul, and the first Apostles and witnesses,
we praise God who has brought us to salvation in Christ
Jesus. In joy we pray: *Honor, love, and praise be yours!*
- We adore you, God, who has saved us in the cross and
  Resurrection of Christ, as we pray . . .
- We are filled with wonder for the good news of
  salvation that is handed on to us from the Apostles
  for the life of the world, as we pray . . .
- We worship you, God, whose Spirit is poured out on
  us in a continual new Pentecost, that we might be
  preachers of the Gospel, as we pray . . .
- We are filled with love for the power of the Spirit
  who moves us beyond human reason to the experience of Jesus as the Christ, as we pray . . .

Closing

Living God, you sent Jesus among us to bring us the gift
of salvation by his cross and Resurrection. Through the
service of Peter, Paul, and the first witnesses and Apos-

tles, the proclamation of the Gospel to all nations and all ages began. Breathe forth your Spirit on us in a new Pentecost that we might proclaim the good news of salvation faithfully in every generation until Christ comes again in glory with the fullness of your Reign. We ask this as all things through Jesus our Messiah forever and ever. Amen.

EVENING

Like the early disciples gathered in the upper room, we are called from our daily labors. So we wait in the night for the coming of the Spirit in a dawn of justice that will never end. The light of Christ flashes in our life, steadily calling us each by name that we might be witnesses of Christ before all the ages. We pray that our thoughts, words, and deeds may be instruments for the spread of the Gospel to all whom we meet.

Call to Prayer

Source of every goodness,
in the nighttime you call us each by name
and bring us into your abundant life,
that we might be servants of your holy will.
This night we give you praise and thanksgiving
for the light of faith in Christ
that descends upon us and urges us in the Spirit
to proclaim the Gospel to all nations and in every age.
Jesus fashions us to be your people, the church,
that we might be one community of faith,
founded on his living body
for the life of the world and the salvation of all.
Your Spirit descends upon us in a new Pentecost
that we might faithfully spread the Good News
as did Peter, Paul, and the first disciples.

Thanksgiving

Saul lay on the ground. It had seemed like a flash of light. In the twinkling of an eye everything that he had thought was true suddenly had given way to something yet unclear, something that blinded everything that had gone before. What was this

Reading

strange whisper that still circled in his ears? He thought he had been doing the right thing, preserving the faith of his ancestors. And now . . . this! Deep inside him he knew his life had changed. Vaguely he remembered the words that now brought him sorrow and joy: "I am Jesus of Nazareth whom you are persecuting." (Acts of the Apostles 9:4–5)

Intercessions   God calls us to proclaim the good news of salvation to all the earth. Knowing that the Spirit will guide us in fidelity we offer our needs to God, as we pray: *Keep us mindful of your love.*

- For the Christian communities, that we may ground our faith in the person of Christ Jesus whose Resurrection is our life, let us pray . . .
- For those who lead us in the faith, that their ministry in the church may mirror the compassion and wisdom of Jesus, let us pray . . .
- For preachers of the Gospel at home and abroad, that the Spirit may grant them insight and courage as they seek to deepen the faith of every disciple, let us pray . . .
- For those who resist the insights of faith, that the spirit of God may gently open their mind and heart to the gift of Gospel truth and freedom, let us pray . . .

Closing   Repeat morning's closing.

Augustine and Monica
Witnesses to the Power
of Christian Conversion

*Augustine (354–430), bishop of Hippo in Africa, is one
of the giants of early Christian thought and spirituality. A
volatile man whose curiosity sent him searching all over for
the meaning of life, his gradual conversion to Jesus Christ
was neither comfortable nor easily sustained. The constant
companion to his endless wandering was his mother, Monica
(c. 331–387), whose tenaciously prayerful and faithful
relationship with her son eventually was blessed by the grace
of his conversion. Both Monica and Augustine provide an
arresting metaphor for the process of Christian conversion.
They represent the strong and undaunting commitment to
personal discovery and acceptance that conversion requires.*

MORNING

Called from darkness to light, we gratefully acknowledge
the Holy Spirit's unending invitation to conversion.
Without question our call to conversion demands openness to new and unexpected opportunities for faith and
to the challenges that these opportunities pose to our
thoughts, words, and deeds. So we pray for the strength
of the Spirit to be made vigilant in prayer as was Monica,
and resolute in our restlessness of heart for Christ as was
her son, Augustine.

Call to Prayer

All praise and glory be yours,
eternal and ever rising light.
You spoke your word of truth
and the clouds of darkness gave way to creation.

Praise

You still speak in our life,
and your Spirit brings us to birth each day.
Before the ages, your Spirit hovered over the woman
and in her womb your eternal Word was made flesh.
In her day, your faithful disciple Monica
was vigilant for the son of her womb
and followed his every path,
praying for your grace to bring him to eternal life.
This day, with Monica and her son,
we are vigilant for that same grace,
living in hope that our life can be emblazoned
with the final grace of your justice and peace.

Reading

Then we went in to my mother, and told her what happened, to her great joy. We explained to her how it had occurred—and she leaped for joy triumphant; and she blessed thee, who art "able to do exceedingly abundantly above all that we ask or think." For she saw that thou hadst granted her far more than she had ever asked for in all her pitiful and doleful lamentations. (Augustine)

Acclamations

In celebration we recall the lives of Monica and Augustine, who prayerfully remind us of the vigilance that our conversion demands. We celebrate their memory, hoping that our life of faith may be ever deepened by the power of the Holy Spirit. In joy we pray: *Honor, love, and praise be yours!*

- We give praise to you, Giver of every gift, whose grace alone can bring us to eternal life, as we pray . . .
- We give thanks for the witness of Monica and Augustine, whose lives are a testimony to the gift of steadfast faith that is the foundation of the Christian family, as we pray . . .
- We are filled with joy at the memory of Augustine and Monica, whose witness gives us hope in the grace of conversion for all, as we pray . . .
- We are grateful for the daily graces of conversion that touch the life of every believer, as we pray . . .

O beauty ever ancient yet ever new, our heart always hungers after you. In the lives of Monica and Augustine, you have given us living witness to your love, which alone can satisfy our restless heart. Stand constantly close to us and never let us be tempted to despair of your passion for us. We ask this as all things through Jesus our Messiah forever and ever. Amen.

Closing

EVENING

The coming darkness is no reason for despair. In our midst the light of Christ burns brightly. With Monica and Augustine, we rejoice at the presence of Christ who always journeys with us, despite the dark places into which we often wander. With all the saints, we rejoice that God desires to lead us home in safety and into the way of peace.

Call to Prayer

Loving and gracious God,
into our life you have poured a marvelous love.
Molded by your hands
you lead our heart to ponder
the meaning of your grace
and to wander on the pathways of life
in search of all the things of beauty
that have been shaped by your provident care.
Yet sometimes our mind and heart
wander without aim or purpose.
Even in these darkest moments,
you dwell ever close,
leading us back to the steadfast safety of your love.
This night we celebrate your loving presence
with Augustine and Monica
whose way you enlightened
until you brought them home.

Thanksgiving

It is not with doubtful but with assured awareness, O Lord, that I love you. You pierced my heart with your Word and I loved you. . . . But what do I love when I love you? . . . I do love a kind of light,

Reading

melody, fragrance, food, embracement when I love
my God; for He is the light, the melody, the fragrance, the food, the embracement of my inner self.
(Augustine)

Intercessions

We remember with joy the testimony of faith and conversion in the lives of Monica and Augustine. With
them we offer our needs to God, as we pray: *Keep us
mindful of your love.*

- For all those who search for truth and beauty, justice
  and peace, that the presence of Christ may make
  them strong in their search, let us pray . . .
- For all those who wander through life looking for the
  grace of fulfillment, that they may open their heart to
  God always with them offering rest, let us pray . . .
- For those who are called to be companions to others
  in their search for spiritual enlightenment and
  refreshment, that the Spirit may guide their ministries, let us pray . . .
- For those who suffer despair in their life's journey,
  that God may send them an angel of peace to be their
  companion in their time of struggle, let us pray . . .

Closing

Repeat morning's closing.

More on Augustine

Chadwick, Henry. *Augustine*. New York: Oxford University Press, 1986.

Warner, Rex, trans. *The Confessions of Saint Augustine:
A New Translation*. New York: New American
Library, 1963.

Patrick of Ireland

Bishop, Missionary,
Symbol of a People's Faith

*Beginning with their subjugation under the English Planta-
genet, the Irish came to rely upon the message of the Gospel
and the church as their light of hope. It is small wonder that
Saint Patrick (389–461), who was kidnapped as an adoles-
cent by pirates from Ireland and held as a slave for six years,
escaped, became a monk, then a bishop and a missionary
back to Ireland, became a symbol of freedom and hope. His
legacy and that of Celtic Christianity continue to enrich the
Christian faith with their focus on the dignity of creation, the
unmerited gift of grace, the blessings of family and community, and the power of hope in the face of oppression.*

MORNING

In the dawn's light, we know that the God of creation is
always present in the rising and falling of every breath
we take. God only wishes peace for the world. Yet God
knows above all others how earth suffers in war and
oppression. With Patrick and all the saints, we join with
peoples everywhere who have suffered from foreign
domination and exploitation to pray for the dawning of
justice and peace in our own time.

Call to Prayer

God of the dawn,
when you formed our body and soul
you molded into the clay of our life
a hunger for peace and a thirst for justice.
You imbued Patrick with the image of Christ
and bade him rise to the invitations of your grace
to bear the message of the Gospel

Praise

to a people who became marked
with the wounds of the Passion.
This day and forever you bid all people,
in the spirit of Patrick's testimony,
to rise up with the gift of your hope
and stand stalwart against the forces of domination
until that day when your victory is final.

Reading

In rising this morning, God's strength guides me. God's power holds me on course. God's wisdom leads me. God's vision sets my direction. God's heart listens to me. God's voice speaks for me. God's embrace protects me. The way of God stretches out before me. (Adapted from "The Breastplate of Saint Patrick")

Acclamations

With Patrick and all the saints, we give praise to God whose bright promise of freedom gives life to every human heart. In joy we pray: *Honor, love, and praise be yours!*
- We adore you, God, whose freedom and justice are fashioned into the human heart, as we pray . . .
- We are filled with wonder at the presence of Jesus, who calls the powerful to the conversion of mercy, as we pray . . .
- We worship you, God, who called Patrick to kindle the fire of the Gospel among the Irish and all the world, as we pray . . .
- We are filled with joy for the legacy of Patrick, whose people give witness to the blessings of strength and hope in the face of oppression, as we pray . . .

Closing

God of truth, with Patrick and all the saints, we pray that you pour out your Holy Spirit upon all the world. Give us the spirit of true prayer and devotion. Bless us with the spirit of justice and mercy. Make us strong to bring your peace to the corners of the world that still search for your light. We ask this as all things through Jesus our Messiah forever and ever. Amen.

Call to Prayer

As the shades of night cross our world, our heart is not dimmed. The lamp of Christ is kindled in our midst with the gift of hope and inspiration. With all the saints, we come to this moment of prayer bearing up to God, in the spirit of Patrick, the names of all those who struggle and hope for a new day of everlasting peace.

Thanksgiving

O God, author and fulfillment of hope,
we come to you this night with praise and thanksgiving
through Jesus our Christ, the light of the world.
You are no God who abandons your people
to the darkness of war and hatred.
As you did with Jesus on the cross,
you stand close to us in human suffering
and see beyond our comprehension.
In your unfathomable plan,
every wound is made a blessing.
This night, with Patrick and all the saints,
we give you praise and thanks for the gift of hope
that gives new strength to our weary limbs
and makes us strong come the morrow
for yet another day to bear your loving mercy and
    kindness
to a world that too often turns away from your Word.

Reading

Christ above, behind, and before us. Christ at left and right hands guiding. Christ in mind and eye and heart. Christ in every word and breath. Christ in every living creature. Christ whose grace breathes hope and life. Christ whose strength makes strong the weak. Christ the dawn of God's own justice. Christ the everlasting light of peace. (Adapted from "The Breastplate of Saint Patrick")

Intercessions | With Patrick and all the saints, we raise our prayers to God who has raised us up to be strong and faithful witnesses to the freedom of the Gospel as we pray: *Keep us mindful of your love.*

- For all the church, that we may stand strong against the evils that rob people of dignity and freedom, let us pray . . .
- For all those who are called to preach the Gospel at home and abroad, that they may know the inspiration of the Spirit in their labors, let us pray . . .
- For the people of Ireland, and for all people that have known oppression and violence, that the spirit of God may lead them to healing and to freedom, let us pray . . .
- For all those who have given in to the seduction of power, greed, and violence, that Jesus may open their eyes to the path of the Gospel, let us pray . . .

Closing | Repeat morning's closing.

More on Saint Patrick

O'Donoghue, Noel Dermot. *Aristocracy of Soul: Patrick of Ireland.* Wilmington, DE: Michael Glazier, 1987.

O'Riordain, John J. *The Music of What Happens: Celtic Spirituality, A View from the Inside.* Winona, MN: Saint Mary's Press, 1996.

Bernard and Norbert, Francis and Dominic

Reformers of the Religious Life

Bernard of Clairvaux (1090–1153), in his Cistercian reforms, called Benedictine communities back to a pristine observation of the Rule. Norbert of Xanten (c. 1080–1134) reformed the life of canons regular who sought to combine traditional religious life with priestly and pastoral ministry. Francis of Assisi (c. 1181–1226) and Dominic (c. 1170– 1221), in the foundation of mendicant orders, raised up evangelical poverty and total availability for ministry as new models for religious men and women. These four reformers witness to the ongoing adaptation and renewal needed by religious communities.

MORNING

Call to Prayer

At the start of this new day, we are reminded that as Christians we are called to give up everything that possesses us save for the love of Christ. Realizing that the vowed life is one of many equal vocations, God's call in our own life is enriched and enlivened by the solidarity of religious in the church with all believers who are seeking to serve Jesus.

Praise

All glory and honor are yours,
O fountain of all holiness,
for from you comes our life and our light.
In every age you raise up women and men
to sing your praises and to move us by their witness
to a greater service of one another.

This day we join our voice with the hosts of heaven
to sing your glory until that final dawn
when every tear shall be wiped away
and every human joy shall be crowned with your goodness.
This day, with those who have vowed their lives to your
    service,
we give you praise
for your holiness sustains us in this world.

Reading

The first purpose for which you have come together
is to live in unity in the house and to be of one mind
and one heart in God. . . . Let all live together in
harmony and love. And, in each other, honor God
whose temples you have become. (Augustine)

Acclamations

We call to mind the life and witness of faith in Bernard
and Norbert, Francis and Dominic. Grateful for their
inspiration for the life of religious communities, we are
mindful of the gift of holiness in our own life. In joy we
pray: *Honor, love, and praise be yours!*
- We adore you, God, who has called all of us to love
  one another and serve one another in prayer and
  mercy, as we pray . . .
- We worship you, God, who calls women and men to
  the life of the counsels for the edification of the
  church, as we pray . . .
- We bless you, God, who has enriched the life of the
  church with the witness of religious communities at
  prayer and in service, as we pray . . .
- We are grateful for the Holy Spirit, whose diverse gifts
  of grace are ever calling us to new depths of conversion of life, as we pray . . .

Closing

God of all holiness, you raise up women and men to
sing your praise and serve all people by a life of poverty,
celibacy, and Gospel obedience. We thank you for the
witness of Bernard and Norbert, Francis and Dominic.
Through the witness of religious communities, enrich
the life of all believers who are seeking your pathway of
holiness in faith and service. Amen.

As the shadows of the night advance, our life is enlightened by the presence of Jesus, who bids us to Gospel living. Realizing that the gift of holiness, given to us in baptism, is made manifest in diverse and marvelous ways, we celebrate with all women and men who have vowed poverty, celibacy, and obedience for the edification of the church. With Bernard and Norbert, Francis and Dominic, we pray for and with all religious that their lives may be blessed by an ongoing conversion of life for the enrichment of the whole people of God.

Call to Prayer

O God, you are the wellspring of all holiness
and the author of all life.
In each age you raise up women and men
to embrace religious life
for the service of the Gospel and the life of the church.
This night we are grateful for the service of those
who have moved your religious to new depths of
    conversion
and called your communities of faith
to new horizons of ministry and service.
With Bernard and Norbert,
with Francis and Dominic,
we give you praise and thanks for the gift of religious life,
which is an instrument of Gospel faith
for the life and conversion of the whole world.
You who fashion every human vocation,
you are blessed this night for the myriad ways
by which your grace of conversion
enlightens the whole world
with rich forms of Christian life and service.

Thanksgiving

O Divine Teacher, grant that I may not so much
    seek to be consoled as to console;
To be understood as to understand;
To be loved as to love;
For it is in giving that we receive;

Reading

It is in pardoning that we are pardoned;
And it is in dying that we are born to eternal life.

(Francis of Assisi)

Intercessions God has raised up religious communities to provide
fitting witness in prayer, service, and the common life.
With all those who have helped religious to hear more
clearly Christ's call in their life, we offer our needs to
the living God, as we pray: *Keep us mindful of your love.*

- For all Christians, that the grace of baptism may well
  up in our life as we seek to discern our own Gospel
  vocations, let us pray . . .
- For all those whose life of prayer and faith is a prophetic gift for the church's holiness, let us pray . . .
- For all those who embrace religious life as their means
  of giving flesh to the grace of baptism, let us pray
  . . .
- For all those who are searching to know where God is
  calling them to serve the needs of others and the
  Gospel, let us pray . . .

Closing Repeat morning's closing.

More on Bernard, Norbert, Dominic, and Francis
Capgrave, John. *The Life of Saint Norbert.* Toronto:
    Pontifical Institute of Mediaeval Studies, 1977.
Daniel-Rops, Henry. *Bernard of Clairvaux.* New York:
    Hawthorn Books, 1964.
Monshau, Michael. *Praying with Dominic.* Winona, MN:
    Saint Mary's Press, 1993.
Stoutzenberger, Joseph M., and John D. Bohrer. *Praying
    with Francis of Assisi.* Winona, MN: Saint Mary's
    Press, 1989.

Hildegard of Bingen
and Aelred of Rievaulx
Medieval Mystics, Reformers

The Dark Ages were actually a time of spiritual ferment. Hildegard of Bingen (1098–1179) was an abbess, a mystic, a preacher of church reform, a liturgical dramatist, an author, a musician, and a medical practitioner. Aelred of Rievaulx (1110–1167) resigned as master of the household of King David of Scotland to become a Cistercian monk. Eventually he became abbot of his monastery and wrote the classic on the spiritual life, On Spiritual Friendship. *Hildegard challenged popes, kings, bishops, and princes to follow a more spiritual, Gospel lifestyle, all the while tending the sick people who came to the monastery, writing music, and living in profound contemplation. Aelred addressed new ways of understanding chaste Christian friendship as a reflection of God's passionate love for the world. Both of these mystics call us to look beyond our narrow view of ourselves, to be fully alive, to use all our powers for the good of humanity and the love of God, and to realize that active love becomes fully effective only when grounded in prayer.*

MORNING

Call to Prayer

As daylight appears, the spirit of God enlightens our mind and heart. The Spirit makes us bold to see new pathways of living the Gospel, of shedding our dark desires to be gods unto ourselves, and of embracing new deeds of goodness. With the coming of this day we pray that we may be courageous enough to follow God's invitations of grace at every moment.

Praise

O God, you have fashioned the human heart and mind,
you are the sole power of our life,
who leads us into the endless day of your justice.
In every age you raise up saints
to be messengers of peace and true disciples of Jesus.
This day we celebrate Hildegard and Aelred.
You touched their lives
and invited them to see new visions and to dream new
    dreams.
With them as our companions,
you make us bold to do the same
so that the Gospel of Jesus may be preached unfettered
by the manacles of fear, bigotry, and sloth.
This day you are praised, O gracious God,
for the unfolding of your infinite love
that is always beyond our comprehension.

Reading

The brightness of God shines in the good works of
just people, so that God can be known, adored, and
worshipped so lovingly on earth, and so that the virtues of these people can embellish the holy city with
their decorations. For by doing good works with the
help of God, people worship God with their countless and wonderful actions. (Hildegard of Bingen)

At the start of this day, we offer our praise to God for those whose lives inspire us to new depths of Gospel living. In joy we pray: *Honor, love, and praise be yours!*

- We adore you, God, who has given us the Gospel of Jesus as the light leading us to new pathways of living, as we pray . . .
- We are filled with praise at the invitations of grace that lead us beyond our fears to the deepening of our life in Christ, as we pray . . .
- We honor you, God, who tumbles our human pride and lifts us, in the Spirit, to dream new dreams and see new visions, as we pray . . .
- We are filled with joy for your mercy, God, who brings an end to human discord and hatred in society, as we pray . . .

God of prophecy and song, you raised up Hildegard of Bingen and Aelred of Rievaulx to sing and speak of your love in ways unseen before their time. With them as our companions in the faith, stretch forth your hand and fashion our life anew, beyond our fears and comforts, so that we may love you and one another as you have loved us without condition or compromise. We ask this as all things through Jesus our Messiah forever and ever. Amen.

As evening falls, we are filled with gratitude for the light of Christ that blazes forth in our midst and puts the shadows of human fear to flight. Together with Hildegard, Aelred, and all the saints, this night we celebrate the victory of Christ that has brought us the gift of salvation to every woman, man, and child without distinction.

O God of dreams and prophecies,
from the shadowed and unexpected corners of our life
your voice is heard anew.
You raise up prophets in our midst
that your Spirit might stretch our life

to the fullness of the Gospel.
This night we give you praise and thanks
for your word that fashions us in friendship
and makes of your creation a community of light
to sing your praises until the night is no more.
You are the power of love itself
drawing us closer to one another in the heart of Christ,
binding up our wounds and bringing us your peace
that knows no end in its joy and passion.

Reading

What happiness, what security, what joy to have someone to whom you dare to speak on terms of equality as to another self. . . . What, therefore, is more pleasant than so to unite to oneself the spirit of another and of two to form one. . . . "A friend," says the Wise Man, "is the medicine of life." Excellent, indeed, is that saying. For medicine is not more powerful or more efficacious for our wounds in all our temporal needs than the possession of a friend who meets every misfortune joyfully, so that, as the Apostle says, shoulder to shoulder, they bear one another's burdens. (Aelred of Rievaulx)

Intercessions

God is friendship. In the friendship of God we are bound as the one Body of Christ. In the spirit of our life in Jesus, we offer our needs to our God, as we pray: *Keep us mindful of your love.*

- For all the churches, that a renewal of ecumenism may see the day when the Body of Christ is healed of all division, let us pray . . .
- For our world community, that the spirit of Gospel friendship may bring an end to war and hostility, let us pray . . .
- For the gift of loving friendship, that our human need for companionship may be crowned with the love of Jesus, let us pray . . .
- For the lonely and those who despair of ever being loved, that we may bring them authentic human warmth and care, let us pray . . .

Repeat morning's closing.

More on Hildegard and Aelred

Durka, Gloria. *Praying with Hildegard of Bingen*. Winona, MN: Saint Mary's Press, 1991.
McGuire, Brian Patrick. *Brother and Lover: Aelred of Rievaulx*. New York: Crossroad, 1994.

Anthony of Padua
Franciscan, Preacher, Man of Prayer

Anthony of Padua (1195–1231) is one of the most beloved saints. His life story mirrors many aspects of the search that is at the heart of anyone's journey of faith. He gave up a life of some means and entered an Augustinian monastery. Later he left the monastic life for the life of a Franciscan friar. One of Anthony's most profound gifts was authentic preaching of the Gospel that begins in the spirit of personal prayer. In this sense, he is the patron of the lost, teaching Christians to discover anew the spirit of prayer that many times can be lost in the rush of modern life.

MORNING

Call to Prayer

God, the dawn breaks into our world again, seeking out the lost and the wayward with the gifts of mercy and tender love. Like a child stealing into his or her parents' room in the morning, you, God, tenderly call us to the gift of this new day. We pray with Anthony and all the saints to be attentive to the invitations of grace that you place before us. May we never lose our way to you.

Praise

God of peace,
we adore your beauty and mercy
and give you praise on this day of salvation.
In the progress of the ages,
you sent to us your beloved, Jesus our Savior,
who taught us with childlike simplicity
the tenderness of your love,
and who taught us with the strength of the cross
the unshakable fidelity of your passion for us.

With Anthony and all the saints,
we give you praise and glory on this day of grace
for the movement of your Spirit in our life
that bids us speak to you in prayer and gentle love.

Reading

Compassion toward our neighbor ought to be three-fold: if he sins against us, we ought to forgive him: "Many sins are cleansed by faith and compassion" (Proverbs 15:27). If he strays from the path of rectitude and truth, we should instruct him: "The person who brings a sinner back from his way will save his soul from death . . ." (James 5:20). If he is in need, we must help him: "Happy is he who has regard for the lowly and the poor" (Psalms 40:2). In this way, we will be "compassionate as [God] is compassionate." (Anthony of Padua)

Acclamations

In the spirit of Anthony of Padua, whose gifts of prayer and preaching continue to enrich God's people, we acclaim the presence of God, who draws us more deeply into the gift of loving. In joy we pray: *Honor, love, and praise be yours!*
- We adore you, God, who has made our heart needy in prayer, as we pray . . .
- We are filled with wonder at the presence of Jesus, who climbs into the arms of our life with the tender love of a child, as we pray . . .
- We honor your name, O God, which puts to flight every spirit of confusion and fear, as we pray . . .
- We are filled with joy of the companionship of Anthony and all the saints, as we pray . . .

Closing

O God, you always seek out the lost and bring home the wayward to your tender mercy and love. As you raised up Anthony of Padua to bring the loving message of Christ to those who were lost, make us children of your goodness and teach us to bear humbly the Word of life to those who are most in need of finding the pilgrim path to your beauty. We ask this as all things through Jesus our Messiah forever and ever. Amen.

EVENING

Call to Prayer

With the coming of the night, there are those in our world who fear losing their way. God does not abandon us, however, but lights the lamp of Christ, who enters our life in childlike love to lead us always home. With Anthony and all the saints, we pray this night in thanksgiving for the presence of the child in our midst who graces our homeward journey with joy and hope.

Thanksgiving

O God of majesty and truth,
into the lives of women and men
you sent your beloved Jesus
to make manifest in the heart of the world,
the heart of your love for all creation.
Jesus walked among us clothed in truth
that your message of everlasting peace
might be given flesh in our midst.
With Anthony and all the saints,
we give you praise and thanks for the gift of Christ,
who does not abandon us to fear and confusion,
but leads us deeply into our heart and soul
that we might find there the tabernacle of your
      presence.
From that place of your dwelling,
you fashion words of thanks
with which we give you praise.

Reading

We beg you, Unity and Trinity,
that the soul which you have created
may safely flee to you
on that last day of affliction and fire,
when the silver rope will be broken.
Welcome it, that freed from the snares of evil,
it may come to you with the freedom
and glory of a child of God.
With your help,
one God in three, who are blessed for all ages. Amen.
                                        (Anthony of Padua)

With Anthony of Padua and all the saints, we raise our needs to you, God, who loves us and stays close to us in every moment of our life, as we pray: *Keep us mindful of your love.*

- For all Christians, that our living of the Gospel may be grounded in a living relationship with Christ, let us pray . . .
- For all preachers and ministers everywhere, that the spirit of God may lead them to speak the word with gentleness and conviction, let us pray . . .
- For all those whose lives are lost, that in the spirit of Saint Anthony, the Spirit may lead them inward to the presence of God in the movements of their heart, let us pray . . .
- For those in ministry, that they may give strong witness to the Gospel, the heart of all the baptized, let us pray . . .

Repeat morning's closing.

More on Anthony of Padua
Hardick, Lothar. *Anthony of Padua: Proclaimer of the Gospel.* Paterson, NJ: Saint Anthony's Guild, 1993.
Nugent, Madeline Pecora. *Praying with Anthony of Padua.* Winona, MN: Saint Mary's Press, 1996.

Clare of Assisi
Founder, Spiritual Guide

Clare of Assisi's (1194–1253) deep friendship with Francis is legendary. Attracted by Francis's original religious vision, Clare gave up a life of privilege and embraced poverty and prayer. Her efforts, with those of Francis, revolutionized religious communities of the thirteenth century. Her community of sisters, the Poor Clares as they came to be called, lived the life of the poor of her time. This community of women freely committed themselves to a life of contemplation and humility in an age when the institutional church was enamored with the political glories of the late Middle Ages and the early Renaissance. Despite her hidden life, nobility and commoners alike sought Clare's spiritual wisdom. The legacy of Clare's life and witness has continued to be a prophetic inspiration to the church and to religious life into our own era.

MORNING

Call to Prayer

As day breaks, God lays before us the grandeur of creation in all its simplicity and elegance. With Clare of Assisi and all the saints, we celebrate the presence of God as we are called to live the simplicity of Christ's Gospel. With joy we pray that Jesus may lead us in new paths of service and prayer for the sake of all the poor of the world.

Praise

God of all creation,
at the dawn of time you formed and nourished
the garden of your delights
and gave the glory of your simple beauty to us.

Christ is the sun of justice who dawns upon us
in the elegance of fields and cities.
This day we give you praise and adoration
for your presence, imprinted in our flesh,
makes us strong for the service of all those
who cry out to you for bread, for love, and for human
    dignity.
This day we give you praise,
celebrate the majesty of your love,
and praise you for the example of Clare's joy in simplicity.

Praying with Clare will help Christians to nurture the life of their soul. Clare gives witness that freeing oneself from acquisitiveness, living simply, and being an empty vessel for God to fill will lead to true peace. . . . No love can be greater than that of Jesus who gave his life to make us sisters and brothers in the human family. (Ramona Miller and Ingrid Peterson)

Reading

With the anticipation of God' graces at this morning hour, with Clare of Assisi and women and men of faith of every age, we praise the God of creation. In joy we pray: *Honor, love, and praise be yours!*
- We adore you, God, who has imprinted the divine image in all of creation, as we pray . . .
- We are filled with joy for the presence of God, who fills us, beyond the things of this world, with the bread that satisfies us without end, as we pray . . .
- We worship you, God, who called Clare to give witness to the wealth of Gospel poverty, as we pray
. . .
- We are filled with hope by the spirit of Clare that witnesses against the powers of greed and war, as we pray . . .

Acclamations

God of humility and love, you raised up your servant Clare to give fitting witness to the power of prayer and the true wealth of Gospel poverty. With her as our companion in the faith, may we always prefer your love

Closing

to the passing infatuations of our mind and changing heart. May we stand with Clare as a fitting witness to the power of Christ's Passion and Resurrection in this life and always. We ask this as all things through Jesus our Messiah forever and ever. Amen.

EVENING

Call to Prayer

In this evening hour, the witness of Clare of Assisi, resolute in the face of invaders, gives us strength and hope. With her as our companion, we are enlightened by the light of Jesus to stand in courage with those who are needy, and in strength against the evil of oppression.

Thanksgiving

O God of love and passion,
you stand close to those who suffer
and those who cower in fear.
In Jesus you have placed into our heart
a light that gives comfort and strength without end.
Just as your servant Clare resolutely stood forward
to confront the powers of hatred and human suffering,
so too do you call us to serve the needs
of all those who despair of Christ's light in this life.
This night we give you praise and thanksgiving
for the salvation that dispels the power of evil.
You are praised this night for the courage you give us
to stand as companions with all those who seek your
    love.
This night we give you thanks
for you never abandon us even when we are tempted to
    despair
at the sound of war's drums or evil's laughter.

Reading

Place your mind before the mirror of eternity!
  Place your soul *in the brilliance of glory!*
Place your heart *in the figure of the* divine *substance!*
  And *transform* your entire being *into the image*
  of the Godhead Itself through contemplation.

So that you too may feel what His friends feel
    as they taste the *hidden sweetness*
that God . . . has reserved from the beginning
    for those who love. . . .

(Clare of Assisi)

Intercessions

With Clare of Assisi and all the saints, we bring the needs of the world before the God who asks us to cast off our selfishness and don the garb of loving service, as we pray: *Keep us mindful of your love.*

- For all Christians, that our life may conform to the simplicity of the Gospel, let us pray . . .
- For all those who follow in the footsteps of Clare and Francis of Assisi, that their gifts of prayer, preaching, and service in the church may be a prophetic leaven of holiness in our midst, let us pray . . .
- For those who are called in social service to tend the needs of the poor, the needy, the sick, and all who suffer, let us pray . . .
- For those who are held in bondage by a spirit of greed and dominance that God might break their chains, let us pray . . .

Closing

Repeat morning's closing.

More on Clare of Assisi

Miller, Ramona, and Ingrid Peterson. *Praying with Clare of Assisi.* Winona, MN: Saint Mary's Press, 1994.

Peterson, Ingrid. *Clare of Assisi: A Biographical Study.* Quincy, IL: Franciscan Press, 1993.

Thomas Aquinas
Theologian and Mystic

Thomas Aquinas (1225–1274) was a man of many passions. Dominican life channeled his passion into a search for, and investigation of, God's love in the world. Unquestionably a genius, a prolific writer, and a deeply emotional man, Aquinas still captures the attention of the world in his ability to build on the secular Aristotelian philosophy of his time to speak to his world about God, Christ, faith, the human condition, and salvation. While in some senses bound to his culture and age, Aquinas serves as a fitting model of the commitment of faith to understanding God's love in experience and in intellectual discovery. Aquinas was also a mystic who, later in life, declared that all of his scholarship was ephemeral compared to the direct union with God experienced in profound contemplation.

MORNING

Call to Prayer

This new day breaks into our life, and the spirit of God rouses our hunger for the love of God. We do not know why. We do not understand. Yet our craving for the presence of Christ grows each day that we live. With Aquinas and all those who seek God, we are strengthened by the Spirit this day to search and yearn for the presence of Christ who alone is drink for our thirst and bread for our hunger.

Praise

O God of intellect and passion,
you have placed into our heart
a hunger and thirst for learning and love.
In this you have made us as yourself,
you who hunger for our love of you.

This day we welcome your Holy Spirit
into our mind and heart,
to invite us again on a quest for your glory,
that we might seek you above all others
as the love for which our heart and body long.
This day the never-ending Son of justice
incites our will and passion,
that we might hunger and thirst for you
as the true object of our loving devotion.

Reading

The light in which we must love our neighbours is
God, for what we ought to love in them is that they
be in God. Hence it is clear that it is specifically
the same act which loves God and loves neighbour.
And on this account charity extends not merely to
the love of God, but also to the love of neighbour.
(Thomas Aquinas)

Acclamations

On this new day, God stirs a spirit of inquiry in our
heart that we might seek divine love above all other
things. In joy we pray: *Honor, love, and praise be yours!*
• We worship you, God, who moves our mind and
  heart to seek the Reign of God above all else, as we
  pray . . .
• We are filled with joy for the spirit of inquiry that is
  itself the presence of the Holy Spirit, as we pray . . .
• We adore you, God, who in Christ never abandons us
  in searching and seeking for the beauty of God's
  Reign, as we pray . . .
• We are filled with wonder and praise for the works
  of humanity wrought through the inspiration of the
  Holy Spirit, as we pray . . .

Closing

Source of wisdom, understanding, and passion, you place
in our soul the quest for your beauty and truth. In your
Spirit, like Thomas Aquinas, we may never cease from
searching for your holy will. Keep us faithful to our
searching and never let the limits of our mind keep us
from knowing the full measure of your truth that indeed
is beyond the prejudice of our present understandings.

We ask this as all things through Jesus our Messiah forever and ever. Amen.

EVENING

Call to Prayer

The God of creation has fashioned us so that our mind continues to wonder and our heart continues to yearn, even into the night. With Thomas Aquinas and teachers of the faith in every age, we invite the light of Christ this night and forever to be our passion and guide to urge us on toward the beauty that is the Reign of God yet to be made full.

Thanksgiving

Fountain of all wisdom and grace,
when you molded our being
from the clay of this earth,
you imprinted into our life and breathed into our soul
an urgency of mind and body
for the brilliance of your justice and peace.
This night the light of Christ inflames our passions,
that we might seek you with ever greater devotion
until that day when your final dawn
fills our mind and heart with your grace.
This night the light of Christ
scatters the darkness of our doubts
and warms us to be faithful to our lifelong struggle
to be embraced by the fullness of your passionate love.

Reading

The object of the will, that is the human appetite, is the Good without reserve, just as the object of the mind is the True without reserve. Clearly, then, nothing can satisfy our will except such goodness, which is found, not in anything created, but in God alone. (Thomas Aquinas)

God has placed into our heart and mind a desire to search endlessly for the one, the true, the beautiful, the good. Knowing the frailties of our human nature, we seek, like Thomas Aquinas, the guidance of the Spirit in our searching, as we pray: *Keep us mindful of your love.*

- For all God's people, that we may be faithful to our search for the face of the Most High and a love of God's ways, let us pray . . .
- For students everywhere, that they may be enlightened by the Spirit and given the grace of appreciation for learning, let us pray . . .
- For theologians and teachers of theology, that God may make them bold for the tasks of inquiry, insight, and new discovery, let us pray . . .
- For those who have been led to new discoveries of the faith, that they may be consoled when their efforts are held in suspicion, let us pray . . .

Repeat morning's closing.

More on Thomas Aquinas

Davies, Brian. *The Thought of Thomas Aquinas.* Oxford, England: Clarendon Press, 1993.

Fatula, Mary Ann. *Thomas Aquinas: Preacher and Friend.* Collegeville, MN: Liturgical Press, 1993.

Thomas Becket
and Thomas More
Defenders of the Gospel in the World of Politics

Christianity has always been in tension with culture. Two great men who gave their lives for the sake of the Gospel's freedom from the subversions of the political order in England were the archbishop of Canterbury, Thomas Becket (1118–1170) and English Chancellor Thomas More (1478–1535). The events surrounding their lives and their martyrdoms were admittedly complex and not necessarily devoid of intrigue and political maneuvering. However, in simplest terms, they refused to collude with their respective monarchs in undermining the unity and freedom of the English church for royal political gain. We do well to admire and emulate their tenacity in upholding the freedom of the Gospel from political manipulation.

MORNING

Call to Prayer

As this new day begins, the Gospel dawns on us in freedom and integrity. With Thomas Becket and Thomas More, we pray for the security of God's people in the world and the mission of the church to preach Christ crucified and risen to a world that would rather worship itself.

Praise

Cornerstone of every nation and people,
you created us in love.
Your Spirit moves among our world
and inspires our ingenuity
so that our societies may reflect your glory.

As we adore the presence of Jesus in our world this day,
we honor the memory of your holy martyrs,
Thomas Becket and Thomas More,
who gave their lives for the freedom of the Gospel
to be spoken in prophecy against greed and manipulation.
Your Spirit moves within us this day
to stand strong against the forces of evil
that seek to undermine the power of your Word
and to bring healing to the sick, bread to the hungry,
and dignity to those who have been brought low.

Reading

Forgive us, O Lord, we acknowledge ourselves as the
   type of the common man,
of the men and women who shut the door and sit by
   the fire;

.   .   .   .

Who fear the injustice of men less than the justice
   of God;
Who fear the hand at the window, the fire in the
   thatch, the fist in the tavern, the push into the
   canal,
Less than we fear the love of God.
                    (Thomas Becket in T. S. Eliot's
                    Murder in the Cathedral)

Acclamations

At the breaking of this new day, we give God thanks for
the martyrs who proclaimed in their life and in their
death the freedom of the Gospel. In joy we pray: *Honor,
love, and praise be yours!*
- We adore you, God, who sealed the gift of freedom
  for us in the Resurrection of Christ, as we pray . . .
- We are filled with wonder at the witness of the martyrs who imitated our Savior even to giving their life
  for others, as we pray . . .
- We worship you, God, who raised up Thomas Becket
  and Thomas More as shining examples of strength
  and courage against the evils of political manipulation and domination, as we pray . . .
- We are filled with joy for the freedom to offer God authentic worship in spirit and in truth, as we pray . . .

Closing | God of all salvation, Jesus walked in the ways of his people, announcing salvation despite the powers that opposed your goodness. In imitation of Christ's integrity and sacrifice, your Spirit inspired Thomas Becket and Thomas More to take up the cross and labor for the freedom of the Gospel. The strength of their convictions united their death to the death of the Savior, their hope to the hope of the Resurrection. Give us the courage to announce boldly your favor and goodness before every people and nation. Amen.

EVENING

Call to Prayer | Though the coming of the night bears with it the shadows of fear, we are warmed by the presence of Jesus, who lights our way toward the final dawn of justice and peace. With Thomas Becket and Thomas More, we pray this night that the spirit of God may make us courageous in every way for the proclamation of the Gospel that sets us free.

Thanksgiving | God of all freedom,
we give you praise and thanks
for the gift of salvation that is ours in Christ.
In the death of Christ, we have died to sin.
In the Resurrection of Christ, we are reborn.
In the coming of Christ again, we are given hope.
With Thomas Becket, Thomas More, and all the martyrs,
we celebrate the freedom of the Gospel
that stands before the powers of this world
and sings of your love despite all threats.
Your Spirit moves again within our heart
and grants us the gift of your courage
to make us good servants
of you and your people.
All praise and thanks to you for our salvation in Christ
that grants us your justice and peace
and that is true light for every nation and people.

They heard Jesus say that he must die. And their hearts were confused and in fear. Yet he assured them that anyone who would follow him must take up the cross. For those who save their lives, will lose them. Those who lose their lives for his sake will save them. It profits us nothing to gain the whole world and lose ourselves in the process. (Matthew 16:24–26)

Before the tribunal of the world, the martyrs proclaim the freedom of the Gospel. Confident that God will make us always faithful witnesses, we bring our needs to God, as we pray: *Keep us mindful of your love.*
- For the church, that we may proclaim God's love and freedom before all the nations regardless of the cost, let us pray . . .
- For the nations, that God's love, peace, and justice may be the foundation of every government, let us pray . . .
- For those who offer their life each day in witness against the forces of evil and domination in our world, let us pray . . .
- For those whose faith is weakened by the spirit of greed, ambition, power, and prestige, that the Spirit may enlighten them to God's grace, let us pray . . .

Repeat morning's closing.

More on Thomas Becket and Thomas More

Bolt, Robert. *A Man for All Seasons: A Play in Two Acts.* New York: Vintage Books, 1962.

Fox, Alistair. *Thomas More: History and Providence.* New Haven, CT: Yale University Press, 1982.

Winston, Richard. *Thomas Becket.* New York: Alfred A. Knopf, 1968.

Catherine of Siena
Dominican Woman, Mystic, Prophet for the Church's Reform

Catherine of Siena (1347–1380) was an Italian, lay Dominican mystic who spent years in her home in solitude and contemplation. Catherine's mystical experiences called her to serve poor people and those in prisons, and urged her to challenge the pope to leave Avignon and return to Rome, to reform his ways and rid the church of the corruption that had become a scandal to the faith. For her many activities, she was made to suffer at the hands of others. From this experience, she spoke intimately of Christ's Passion in her life. Catherine of Siena is an important model for prayerful conversion of every Christian and the institutional church.

MORNING

Call to Prayer

Each day the fabric of our life is exposed before the living God, who wishes always to rethread our faith in conversion of life. With Catherine of Siena and all the saints, we enter this new day asking that the spirit of God reform us and all the church for the glory of the Gospel and the salvation of the whole world.

Praise

Gracious and loving God,
from your heavenly dwelling place
you bend toward the earth and call each of us by name.
In this morning hour,
our ears are opened by your Spirit,
that we might hear you calling to us in prayer
and rousing us to meet your invitations of grace.

Like those who love each other passionately,
you burn within us like the rising sun of your love
that our life may be fired in the strength of your glory.
This day, with Catherine of Siena and all the saints,
we hear your voice and open our life
to do your holy will for the life of the world.

Reading

Catherine's active life and mystical experience
cannot actually be separated. What she experienced
in her prayer led her to reach out to sick and sinful
people, to arbitrate disputes, and to seek reform in
the church. Her daily activities were present in her
prayer, and at the same time her prayer and contemplation were present in her activities to the extent
that she often prayed in the middle of what she was
doing or saying. (Patricia Mary Vinje)

Acclamations

Knowing that ongoing conversion of life and prayer are
at the heart of our discipleship in Jesus, we join with
Catherine of Siena and all the saints to give praise to
God this day. In joy we pray: *Honor, love, and praise be
yours!*
- We adore you, God, whose love in our life burns
  within us and moves us to deepen our life in Christ,
  as we pray . . .
- We are filled with joy for the presence of Jesus in our
  life, who calls us from sin to new pathways of grace,
  as we pray . . .
- We worship you, God, who called Catherine of Siena
  to witness to the need for the reform of the church in
  every age, as we pray . . .
- We are filled with love for the spirit of Jesus, who bids
  us to serve poor people and those in suffering, as we
  pray . . .

Closing

O God, your love renews our discipleship in Christ. You
raised up Catherine of Siena, disciple of Saint Dominic
and prophet of Christian reform, to teach us again to
pray, to serve, and to enter into the spirit of ongoing
conversion. With her as our companion, open the heart

of the whole church to the prompting of the Spirit that
everything that is not of you may be burned within us,
and that everything that is of you may flower in our
midst for the good of others. We ask this as all things
through Jesus our Messiah forever and ever. Amen.

EVENING

Call to Prayer

Confident that Christ leads us to new depths of discipleship, we join this night with Catherine of Siena and all
the saints to pray for the ongoing reform and renewal of
the people of God throughout the world. We pray for an
increase of prayer, of service, and of ongoing conversion
of life.

Thanksgiving

Fire of all loving,
this night we offer you praise and thanksgiving
for the gifts you have given us this day in Christ.
We open our sinful heart before you,
knowing that your Spirit of life redeems us
and rescues us from our ways.
This night you burn before us in the light of Christ,
whose gentle presence in our midst
helps us see the pathways of grace
on which you bid us walk for your glory
and the salvation of all those in need.
Your Spirit calls your church to new vigilance,
that we might shed every vain glory from ourself
and see in the message of the Gospel
the only garb of lasting beauty and peace.

Reading

If we were to ask that gentlest most loving young
Man [how to know God's will], . . . this is how he
would answer us: "Dearest children, if you wish to
discover and experience the effects of my will, dwell
within the cell of your soul.". . . As we focus there
the eye of the free will God has given us, we see and
know that his will has become nothing other than
our sanctification.

For as we understand, so we love, and when we love, we find ourselves united with the transformed in love, in this mother charity. (Catherine of Siena)

The spirit of God presses our face to the window of faith so that we might see our life and God's will clearly. With Catherine of Siena and prophets of reform in every age, we pray for the health of our soul and of the church, as we pray: *Keep us mindful of your love.*

- For the church, that the people of God may place the will of God before our own needs, let us pray . . .
- For all the disciples of Jesus, that we may be open to the prompting of the Spirit, who steadily calls us to newness of life and service in Christ, let us pray . . .
- For the Dominican communities and in thanksgiving for the graced contributions of religious women in the ongoing conversion of God's people, let us pray . . .
- For leaders in the church, that they may be models of spiritual reformation for the Body of Christ and for the whole world, let us pray . . .

Intercessions

Repeat morning's closing.

Closing

More on Catherine of Siena
Noffke, Suzanne, trans. *Catherine of Siena: The Dialogue*. New York: Paulist Press, 1980.
Vinje, Patricia Mary. *Praying with Catherine of Siena*. Winona, MN: Saint Mary's Press, 1990.

Ignatius of Loyola
Founder of the Society of Jesus

In the sixteenth century, a seriously wounded Spanish soldier pondered the direction of his life as his wounds healed. The spirit of God stirred as he reached for the Scriptures and the accounts of the lives of the saints. A man of arms was trans-formed into a disciple of Jesus who would provide a revolution in Christian spirituality, scholarship, religious life, and service of the poor for a needy church. The influence of Ignatius of Loyola (1491–1556) has been felt in every corner of Christian life and world history. Besides the Spiritual Exercises, saints, scholars, missionaries, and prophets have been the legacy of Ignatius. Ever adaptive to the times, Ignatius's Jesuit community has been a rich resource for Christians seeking ongoing conversion of life in Jesus.

MORNING

Call to Prayer

On this new day, God calls each of us to newness of life. No thread of our life can escape from the love of God, who fashioned us for the greater honor and glory of God. With Ignatius of Loyola, we offer our whole life to God this day in prayer and in service.

Praise

Blessed are you, O God of all life,
for the new dawn of your love
that is forever breaking into our world.
In each age you call us into the heart of Jesus,
where your light casts out all fear, despair,
selfishness, and doubt,
and where we are warmed into rebirth.
This day your Word glows before us
and beckons us to new depths

of prayer and service to our sisters and brothers.
With Ignatius of Loyola and all the holy ones,
we give you praise and adoration
for the gift of Jesus,
who has freed us from sin
by the power of the Resurrection.

Take, Lord, and receive all my liberty, my memory, **Reading**
my understanding, and my entire will, all that I have
and possess. You have given all to me. To you, Lord,
I return it. All is yours. Dispose of it wholly accord-
ing to your will. Give me your love and your grace.
That is enough for me. (Ignatius of Loyola)

This is the day of our salvation. This day God calls us **Acclamations**
more deeply into the divine will for the glory of God's
name and the salvation of the world. In joy we pray:
Honor, love, and praise be yours!
- We worship you, God, who calls each of us to ongoing conversion of life, as we pray . . .
- We are filled with joy for the life and witness of
  Ignatius of Loyola that has enriched the church and
  the world, as we pray . . .
- We honor you, God, who gives us always a needy
  spirit, a new wisdom, and a new heart for loving, as
  we pray . . .
- We are filled with wonder for the ways you, God,
  invite us to see the Gospel in new ways, as we pray
  . . .

Eternal God of all reason and love, yours are our days **Closing**
and evenings. With Ignatius of Loyola as our companion
in the faith, you invite us to peer into the mirror of our
life to see those horizons to which you beckon us as
disciples of Jesus. Calm our fears and open our heart and
mind. Give us the strength to surrender our life into
your hands for the glory of your name and the salvation
of the whole world. We ask this as all things through
Jesus our Messiah forever and ever. Amen.

EVENING

Call to Prayer

In this evening hour, we surrender our life into the embrace of Christ, who warms us with comfort, hope, and promise. We pray this night that the light of Christ may always burn within us and strengthen us, like clay in a kiln, to be vessels of goodness for those who are in need.

Thanksgiving

O God of all time and space,
in the seasons of our life you are always present,
steadily drawing us to grace and goodness.
Jesus, your beloved and our Savior,
stands in our midst bearing your light of peace
and giving us comfort in our darkness.
Your Spirit moves within us
with the quiet of a nightfall
and the strength of a mother's love.
This night, O most holy Trinity,
we give you praise and thanksgiving
for your loving presence,
which is our joy and lasting peace.

Reading

To bind oneself more to God our Lord and to show oneself generous toward Him is to consecrate oneself completely and irrevocably to His service. . . .

The more one binds himself to God our Lord and shows himself more generous toward His Divine Majesty, the more will he find God more generous toward himself and the more disposed will he be to receive graces and spiritual gifts which are greater each day. (Ignatius of Loyola)

Intercessions

In the Garden of Gethsemane Jesus surrendered his life into the Divine Will. With Ignatius and all the saints, we ask for the strength to follow in Jesus' pathway of surrender, as we pray: *Keep us mindful of your love.*

• For all Christians, that the spirit of God may make us strong to turn our will and our life into the hands of Christ, let us pray . . .

- For every nation and people, that our pursuit of science and art may further human progress and the freedom of every human being, let us pray . . .
- For the Society of Jesus and for all those who find in Jesuit spirituality a pathway to grace, let us pray . . .
- For those whose burdens distract them from listening to the inner voice of God calling them to a newness of purpose, let us pray . . .

Repeat morning's closing.

More on Ignatius of Loyola
Bergan, Jacqueline Syrup, and Marie Schwan. *Praying with Ignatius of Loyola*. Winona, MN: Saint Mary's Press, 1991.
De Dalmases, Candido. *Ignatius of Loyola, Founder of the Jesuits: His Life and Work*. Saint Louis, MO: Institute of Jesuit Sources, 1985.

Martin Luther
Reformer of the Church

*Like the individual, the church is always in need of reform
and conversion. Martin Luther (1483–1546) first learned
this in an Augustinian monastery. All our life is meant to be
centered upon the living Word alone. We are saved by faith
alone. Our good works are a response to that primary gift of
salvation. The ecumenical movement has taught us to appreciate the insights that Luther added to Christian tradition.
Luther would have been much more at home in the Catholic
church of our time. If we are tempted to live as if our work is
central to salvation, we would do well to make Luther's
insights part of our own ongoing conversion as individuals
and as members of the Body of Christ, the church.*

MORNING

Call to Prayer

In the grand simplicity of the dawn, the spirit of God
calls us deeper into the mystery of the heart of Christ.
We are invited to a level of conversion where our life is
meant to become more centered upon the living Word
that brings us salvation through the gift of faith. With
Martin Luther and prophets of every age, we pray this
day that we may have the courage to go where Christ is
leading us.

Praise

O God from whom all things draw life,
though we sin,
you have given the light of salvation to us
and have called us to find our joy in your Word alone.
With Martin Luther and with prophets of every age,
we listen for the sound of your call
that our life might find new vigor and strength

to sing of your goodness
and bear the Good News of salvation
to every living creature.
God of amazing grace,
you alone are the source of our joy
and the giver of every good thing.
To you alone belongs the power and the glory!

Reading

I believe that God created me and all that exists.
He has given me and still preserves
my body and soul with all their powers.

He provides me with food and clothing, home and
family, daily work, and all I need from day to day.
God also protects me in time of danger and guards
me from every evil.

All this he does out of fatherly and divine goodness
and mercy, though I do not deserve it.
Therefore I surely ought to thank and praise, serve
and obey him.
This is most certainly true.

(Martin Luther)

Acclamations

As day breaks, the word of God breaks into our life
anew. We are made bold by the Spirit to ground our life
on the Word alone. In joy we pray: *Honor, love, and
praise be yours!*
- We worship you, God, who made all things by the
  power of the Word of life alone, as we pray . . .
- We are filled with joy for the salvation that is ours as
  a free gift of faith from the author of all grace, as we
  pray . . .
- We adore you, God, who knows that we are sinners,
  unable on our own to be saved, and yet extends to us
  the gift of life, as we pray . . .
- We are filled with joy for the gift of Christ in our
  midst, who calls us to serve one another in peace and
  justice, as we pray . . .

Closing

Author of all life, the fire of your holy Word warms our heart. Your Word burns away our sinfulness and makes us strong to do your will. With Martin Luther and all the prophets, center us more deeply in Christ, that our whole life may be an act of praise for your salvation, which we do not deserve yet that is ours by your gift. We ask this as all things through Jesus our Messiah forever and ever. Amen.

EVENING

Call to Prayer

At the end of this day, we sing praise to God as did the Mother of Jesus at the presence of the Word in her heart and in her womb. With Martin Luther and all God's holy ones, we pray that the presence of Christ within us may be given flesh in our words and deeds that themselves spread the light of Christ, who alone is the salvation of the whole world.

Thanksgiving

O God, you who fashion praise from every creature,
without you we are nothing,
and we have no cause for joy.
You have planted the seed of your Word within us,
and thereby have given the gift of salvation to the world.
This night and forever we give you praise and thanks
for the presence of Christ in our midst,
who scatters the darkness of sin and oppression
and calls every nation to the brilliant glory
of faith, life, and freedom.
Gathered from the dark corners of the earth,
we are warmed by the light of your Word
that alone is the source of life itself.

Reading

Therefore we must here give heed to Mary's last word, which is "God." She does not say, "My soul magnifies itself" or "exalts me." She does not desire herself to be esteemed; she magnifies God alone and gives all glory to Him. She leaves herself out and ascribes everything to God alone, from whom she received it. For though she experienced such an exceeding great work of God within herself, yet she was ever minded not to exalt herself above the humblest mortal living. (Martin Luther)

The Word of God alone brings us salvation. Nothing in our life has merited God's grace. In the spirit of gratitude for God's unmerited gift of salvation in our life, we offer our needs to God, as we pray: *Keep us mindful of your love.*

Intercessions

- For the whole church, that the spirit of ongoing conversion may be at the heart of our witness in Christ, let us pray . . .
- For the spirit of ecumenism, that the Spirit may bring an end to the divisions among the Christian communities, let us pray . . .
- For those who are closed to the presence of God in their life, that the Spirit may open their heart to the Word of life, let us pray . . .
- For those who are called to preach the Good News, that Christ may enlighten their mind, their heart, and the words in their mouth, let us pray . . .

Repeat morning's closing.

Closing

More on Martin Luther
Bainton, Roland. *Here I Stand: A Life of Martin Luther.* New York: Abingdon Press, 1978.

Teresa of Ávila and John of the Cross
Reformers and Renewers of the Christian Spiritual Life

The sixteenth century was an age of intellectual and spiritual reform, renewal, and reimagining. Two spiritual giants gave new life to the soul of the church: Teresa of Ávila (1515–1582) and John of the Cross (1542–1591). Members of the Carmelite order, Teresa and John were touched in a special way by the Spirit that led to their own ongoing conversion of life. Their desire to live solely for God prompted them to reform the Carmelite community. Even though both saints had many demands placed upon them, their mystical experiences fed their souls and have been influential in the ways that Christians have come to understand and practice prayer in the centuries since their deaths.

MORNING

Call to Prayer

With the coming of this new day, God's spirit wakes us from our sleep to the task of ongoing conversion of life. Realizing that there can be no Christian commitment not grounded in a passionate love of God and neighbor, cultivated by intense prayer and selfless service, we enter into the spirit of prayer this day so that God might call all women and men to a renewal of life in Jesus.

Praise

O God, you are the fountain of all love
and the beauty for which our soul yearns.
In every age you speak your word in our life
and draw us more deeply into your heart.

This day we give you praise and adoration
for the fire of your Holy Spirit
that brings light to our darkness
like the rising sun burning away the morning dew.
With Teresa of Ávila and all the saints,
we give you praise for the presence of Jesus
who teaches us the pathway of prayer
that draws us closer to God.

Reading

Whoever has not begun the practice of prayer, I beg for the love of the Lord not to go without so great a good. . . . If one perseveres, I trust then in the mercy of God, who never fails to repay anyone who has taken Him for a friend. For mental prayer in my opinion is nothing else than an intimate sharing between friends; it means taking time frequently to be alone with Him who we know loves us. (Teresa of Ávila)

Acclamations

With Teresa of Ávila and all the saints, we are grateful for the presence of Christ in our life, who draws us deeper into the interior castle of faith until we meet our Holy Friend face-to-face. In joy we pray: *Honor, love, and praise be yours!*

- We adore you, God, who constantly calls us deeper into the life of salvation, as we pray . . .
- We are filled with wonder at our Divine Friend, who touches the dryness of our spirit and refreshes us with every grace, as we pray . . .
- We honor you, God, for you do not abandon us to the frail limits of our human understanding, as we pray . . .
- We are filled with joy by you, God, who raises our thoughts and heart into the grace of prayer and contemplation, as we pray . . .

Closing

Beloved, you fashioned us in love, and you grace us always with the Resurrection of Christ. You raised up Teresa of Ávila and John of the Cross to continue to teach your faithful people the art of authentic prayer and service. Move your Spirit in our midst. Teach us always to pray. Keep us mindful of your presence, Holy Friend, until we meet you at last face-to-face. We ask this as all things through Jesus our Messiah forever and ever. Amen.

EVENING

Call to Prayer

With a mother's tender love, God lights up the house of faith and does not abandon us to darkness. Knowing that we often must walk in a dark night of the soul, God is ever with us to give us courage until the day breaks again. With all the saints, we pray this night to be faithful in our vigil for that final day when the beauty of God's face shall break through the veil of our limited human understanding.

Thanksgiving

O passionate God,
your brilliant light blazes forth,
and you flood our soul with warmth.
Even when we wander away from you,
it is really your face that we are seeking,
your passion for which we groan.
This night you have kindled in our midst
the lamp of Christ,
who is our joy and our love.
Jesus, your beloved, caresses us with your grace
and fills the emptiness of our aching heart.
This night we give you thanks
for you do not abandon us to loneliness
but fill us with pure joy in Jesus, your beloved.
All praise and thanks to you, O lover of the human
    heart!
All praise for your love that makes us whole.

Reading

Love is the soul's inclination, strength, and power in making its way to God, for love unites it with God. The more degrees of love it has, the more deeply it enters into God and centers itself in [God]. . . .

We can compare the soul in its ordinary condition in this state of transformation of love to the log of wood that is ever immersed in fire, and the acts of this soul to the flame that blazes up from the fire of love. The more intense the fire of union, the more vehemently does this fire burst into flames. The acts of the will are united to this flame and ascend, carried away and absorbed in the flame of the Holy Spirit. (John of the Cross)

Intercessions

With John of the Cross, Teresa of Ávila, and all the saints, we offer our needs to the God who draws us always into the fire of Christ's heart for us, as we pray: *Keep us mindful of your love.*

- For all Christians, that our lives may be imbued with the spirit of prayer and contemplation, let us pray . . .
- For all who teach the art of prayer and all who direct the care of souls, that the spirit of God may be their guide and wisdom, let us pray . . .
- For the members of the Carmelite communion, in thanks for their witness to the tradition of prayer, let us pray . . .
- For those who have entered into the dark night of the soul and are tempted to despair, that Christ may be their companion and hope, let us pray . . .

Closing

Repeat morning's closing.

More on Teresa of Ávila and John of the Cross

Broughton, Rosemary. *Praying with Teresa of Ávila.* Winona, MN: Saint Mary's Press, 1990.

Simsic, Wayne. *Praying with John of the Cross.* Winona, MN: Saint Mary's Press, 1993.

Kateri Tekakwitha
Native American Witness
to a Universal Gospel Faith

Kateri Tekakwitha (c. 1656–1680) is a profound example of a Christian trying to balance native cultural traditions and her faith. Kateri was the orphaned daughter of a Mohican father and an Algonquin mother. The smallpox that took away her family left her with damaged eyesight and a disfigured face. Eventually she was baptized by Jesuit missionaries. Shunned by many in her village because of her new faith, she trekked to Sault Sainte Marie, a Christian Indian village close to Montreal. She ministered among her people until her death. Her abiding spiritual legacy is a testimony to the universality of the Gospel that can never be linked only to one people or culture. The Word of life is always able to be incarnated in every human experience and lifestyle.

MORNING

Call to Prayer

The dawn breaks in the forests and on the prairies, bringing the blessings of a new day to every people and nation. Grateful for the Word of life that sustains us, we join with Kateri Tekakwitha and all the saints in celebration of the Gospel of Christ that is good news to all people everywhere.

Praise

God of forest and field,
the earth breaks forth in this new day
to celebrate your living presence
in the movements of nature's seasons
and in the pulsing of the world's heart.

You are the God who fashions praise
even from the rocks and streams,
from living things and plants that grow.
From the clay of this earth you formed all people
and gave the gift of life to every nation.
With Kateri Tekakwitha and all the saints,
we give you praise for the Gospel of life
that does not destroy the beauty of the world's cultures,
but celebrates the power of your creative spirit
through their wondrous variety.

> There, far off, my Sun Father arises, ascends the
>   ladder, comes forth from his place.
> May all complete the road of life, may all grow old.
> May the children inhale more of the sacred breath of
>   life.
> May all my children have corn that they may
>   complete the road of life.
>   ("Invocation to the U'Wannami")

Reading

The glory of God pulses in the heart of all believers at the start of this day. We offer our praise to God for the rich diversity of cultures and expressions of faith in the spirit of the Gospel. In joy we pray: *Honor, love, and praise be yours!*

Acclamations

- We worship you, God, who called Kateri Tekakwitha as an example of Christian conversion among a people new to the Gospel's message, as we pray . . .
- We are filled with wonder at the vitality of the Gospel among diverse peoples and nations, as we pray . . .
- We worship you, God, whose presence is felt among all people, nations, and cultures, as we pray . . .
- We are filled with joy for the presence of the Spirit, who redeems us and binds us as one family for God, as we pray . . .

God of every heart, the Gospel of life is preached in every age that all the nations might come to embrace you. You raised up Kateri Tekakwitha as an example of conversion into the person of Jesus in a land new to the Word.

Closing

Send your Spirit among us that we might continue to preach the Gospel so that your peace may come to rest gently on all nations and cultures. Amen.

EVENING

Call to Prayer | The moon and stars rise over field and forest, over city and village. With the rising of the stars, hope springs up that the Gospel of life might bind all people as God's one community of faith. With Kateri Tekakwitha and all the saints, we pray this night in thanksgiving for the gifts that each culture brings under the Reign of Christ's rising beauty and majesty.

Thanksgiving | O God, you are the all-powerful one
whose beauty is reflected in the majesty of nature.
We give you thanks and praise
for the salvation brought by Christ Jesus.
His true word affirms the rhythms of new cultures
and crowns each human community
with the blessings of peace and promise.

This night we confess how limited our heart is
when we refuse to see your glory grown full
in all people, no matter how different from ourselves.
Tonight your Spirit bids us to look again
and listen to your words
spoken by any believer
no matter the color of their skin, the manner of their
    dress,
the language in which the Good News is proclaimed.
With Kateri Tekakwitha and all the saints,
we give you praise for the boundless nature of your love
that spreads across the earth.

Reading

Fair is the white star of twilight,
And the moon roving
To the sky's end;
But she is fairer, better worth loving,
She, my heart's friend.

("The Heart's Friend")

Intercessions

With Kateri Tekakwitha and all the saints, we offer our
needs to the Creator in the hope that God will open our
heart and mind to all people as children of the one God,
as we pray: *Keep us mindful of your love.*
- For the church, that we may be faithful to the preser-
  vation of native peoples in our preaching of the Gospel to all the world, let us pray . . .
- For all the nations, that the power of greed and domination may be broken in our relations in the global
  community, let us pray . . .
- For missionaries, that they may be given the courage
  to understand those to whom God sends them, let us
  pray . . .
- For those in cultures who are hearing the Gospel for
  the first time, that they may be inspired to find ways
  to allow the message of Jesus to grow within them, let
  us pray . . .

Closing

Repeat morning's closing.

Elizabeth Ann Bayley Seton

Wife, Mother, Religious Educator, Founder, First American Saint

Elizabeth Ann Seton, nee Bayley (1771–1821), began her life in New York social circles. The death of her young husband left her with five children but started her on a journey that led from the Church of England to Roman Catholicism. At the initiative of Bishop John Carroll, she moved to Baltimore and founded the Sisters of Charity, a religious community of women who have made enormous contributions to health care ministry and Catholic education. Elizabeth Seton is considered a founder of the American Catholic school system. During her life, Mother became the title for this strong and tender, sensitive and determined, woman. In 1975 Mother Seton became the first native-born American citizen to be canonized.

MORNING

Call to Prayer

We come to this moment of prayer with Mother Seton as our companion, begging that the spirit of God will make us open to new invitations of grace. With Jesus in our midst, we are confident that we can make this journey of faith in which God will undoubtedly ask of us things we never before dreamed or dared.

Praise

O God, whose voice calls to every human heart,
in each day you make known your will
and you give your creatures courage and strength
to do the good and thereby give you praise.

This day we give you the gift of our adoration
for the ways your grace appears in our life.
Jesus, your beloved, is with us always
guiding us into the depths of your holy will.
With Mother Seton and all the saints,
you make us bold to embrace your Word of life
that you bid us proclaim for the salvation of the world
and the good of every human heart.
Your Spirit stirs within us to see new visions,
to dream new dreams,
and to walk new pathways of service
for the life of your holy people.

Reading

It is true the Journey is long, the burthen is heavy—
but the Lord delivers his faithful servants from all
their troubles. . . . Is it nothing to sleep serene
under his guardian wing—to awake to the brightness
of the glorious sun with renewed strength and
renewed blessings . . . to be assured that love is
enough to tie us faithfully to him. (Elizabeth Ann
Seton)

Acclamations

In this new day, we rejoice at the presence of Christ,
who urges us to new pathways of grace for the service of
God and others. In joy we pray: *Honor, love, and praise
be yours!*

- We adore you, God, who calls us to new ways of serving others and always sustains us in grace to accom-
  plish the works of faith, as we pray . . .
- We are filled with wonder for your graces, God, given
  to us for the life of the church and the glory of your
  name, as we pray . . .
- We worship you, God, who comforts us in our sorrow
  and makes of life's wounds fertile ground for new
  avenues of loving care for others, as we pray . . .
- We are filled with love for the power of Christ that
  transforms obstacles in our life and strengthens us in
  holiness and ministry, as we pray . . .

Closing

O God, who orders the movements and seasons of our life, you raised up Mother Seton in a new land to bear the love of the Gospel to those who sought knowledge and health. Teach us by her example to do as Jesus did among us. Make us servants of your will, never fearful to walk in the pathways of grace you place before us, and ever ready to put our needs aside that others might have life and have it in abundance. Amen.

EVENING

Call to Prayer

At this evening hour, God draws us from our daily labors. We open our heart and make for God a new family not of blood and lineage, but of wisdom and human compassion. We pray this night that we, like Mother Seton, might be encouraged by the Holy Spirit to build for God new families of faith for the proclamation of the Gospel and for the good of every human heart.

Thanksgiving

O God, to you all praise and thanks are given
for you have gathered your human family
to be founded upon your compassion and care.
Jesus, you raised us in the Resurrection,
and become the cornerstone of our lives with one
    another:
lives meant to be lived in peace and justice,
in mercy and provident love.
This night your Spirit burns brightly in our midst,
urging us onward to a new day of justice,
when every heart shall be quieted in your love,
and every question shall be calmed with your
    understanding.
This night we confess your name, O Holy One of Israel,
for the goodness you give to us
that we might give that same gift to one another.

Reading

Dropping asleep with my crucifix under my pillow
and the Blessed Virgin's picture pressed on my heart,
Kit and Rebecca [her daughters] fast asleep near me

—think of the contrast, to wake with the sharpest lightnings and loudest thunder. . . .

I crept away to the choir window, to see what had become of my little peaceable Queen [the moon], who was wrapped in clouds . . . while she was tak[ing] her quiet course above them.

There again I found the soul which fastens on God. Storms or whirlwinds pass by or over it, but cannot stop it one moment. (Elizabeth Ann Seton)

Intercessions

No human heart is exempt from the trials of earthly life. Confident that the presence of God sustains us always, we bear the needs of our human family to the One who gives us hope and peace, as we pray: *Keep us mindful of your love.*

- For the church, that God might lead us to new pathways of service for the spread of the Gospel and the good of the human family, let us pray . . .
- For all the nations, that those who lead us in civil government may hear the cries of the poor and enact laws that bring comfort to the afflicted, let us pray . . .
- For those who minister to God's people in education and in the care of the sick, that their service may be graced with strength, wisdom, and compassion, let us pray . . .
- For the Sisters of Charity and the Daughters of Charity, that their service of God's people in the United States may be an inspiration to the people of this land to build for God a house founded on love and mercy, let us pray . . .

Closing

Repeat morning's closing.

More on Mother Seton

Alderman, Margaret, and Josephine Burns. *Praying with Elizabeth Seton.* Winona, MN: Saint Mary's Press, 1992.

Melville, Annabelle M. *Elizabeth Bayley Seton, 1771–1821.* New York: Charles Scribner's Sons, 1976.

William Penn
and John Woolman
Quakers, Pioneers,
and Peacemakers

Sensitive to the persecution of his Society of Friends (Quakers) community in England, William Penn (1644–1718) set sail for the New World to found the colony that evolved into the Commonwealth of Pennsylvania. Such a venture for religious freedom could only have been born from a profound faith, arising from an intimate relationship with Christ. Another Quaker, John Woolman (1720–1772), followed in Penn's footsteps. Woolman's Journal is a classic recounting of the enduring power of God in a devout person's life. It also tells of Woolman's ministry of peacemaking and freeing the slaves. As Quakers, Penn and Woolman knew the depths of quiet prayer where they encountered the Inner Light. Their example and that of the Quaker community as a whole are prophetic gifts to our world, which desperately needs to seek God's voice in quiet so as to wield the only effective weapon in the face of evil, God's peace.

MORNING

Call to Prayer

As dawn breaks, the quiet of the morning invites us gently to listen for the voice of God—the Inner Light—moving in our life. Seeking God as the center of our being, we pray this day with William Penn and John Woolman that our actions may be founded upon that peace and serenity that come from Christ alone.

Gentle and loving God,
you speak to us in the quiet of our heart,
and you enlighten our mind
with thoughts of everlasting peace.
While the nations rage in folly,
you move among us with invisible grace
planting in our heart the Spirit's bold courage
to go forth and make of our lands and cities
a colony of peace and justice for the oppressed.
With William Penn, John Woolman,
and lovers of peace everywhere,
we praise the majesty of your name,
and we offer our body and soul to you this day
that in the works of our mind and hands
we might proclaim your quiet goodness—
goodness that flows to all the world
from the heart of Jesus.

Praise

In the Lord Jehovah is everlasting strength, and as
the mind by a humble resignation is united to Him
and we utter words from an inward knowledge that
they arise from the heavenly spring, though our way
may be difficult and require close attention to keep
in it, . . . yet if we continue in patience and meek-
ness, heavenly peace is the reward of our labors.
(John Woolman)

Reading

In the quiet of the morning, God turns us toward that
peace that is beyond all understanding and that flows to
us from Jesus. In joy we pray: *Honor, love, and praise be
yours!*

Acclamations

- We adore you, God, for Christ has brought us peace
  in the the cross and glorious Resurrection, as we pray
  . . .

- We are filled with wonder at the miracle of redemption that we sense in quiet prayer and that urges us to
  service in Christ's name, as we pray . . .
- We worship you, God, who moved William Penn,
  John Woolman, and lovers of religious liberty to found
  new homes for those in search of Gospel freedom, as
  we pray . . .

- We are filled with joy for the heritage of liberty that moves us to extend the welcome of Jesus to those whose lives are still haunted by the specters of oppression and fear, as we pray . . .

Closing

Bathed in the light of Jesus Christ, William Penn led his people to a new land in search of religious liberty and the freedom to follow Christ's Gospel path. John Woolman led his sisters and brothers to peaceful ways and worked to abolish the abomination of slavery. Send forth your Spirit upon us that we, like them, might be opened to your holy will. Help us listen to our inner voice that we might be your peace. Amen.

EVENING

Call to Prayer

In the cool of the evening, God walks among us. Beneath the sounds of the world coming to night's time of rest, the voice of God speaks to us from the ineffable vision of Christ's light in our soul. We pray this night that our ears might be open and our eyes widened for the vision of faith that is the promise of God's peace grown full in our midst. God light the flames of our inner light.

Thanksgiving

God who is light and peace,
when the first disciples gathered in fear,
Jesus appeared in their midst
and spoke to them of your gift of peace, your shalom.
This night we give you thanks and praise
for the gift of your shalom that is spoken once again.
In a world of passing lights,
the vision of your peace is the one lamp
that can lead our world into the dawn
of true justice and mercy.
Without Christ's light of peace,
we lose our way and sink back into fear.
With William Penn, John Woolman,
and lovers of peace everywhere,
we are grateful this night for the power of your Spirit

that leads us through the darkness
toward that everlasting glory of your Reign,
the life for which our heart yearns
in the quiet of our evenings and our mornings.

Reading

To consider mankind otherwise than brethren, to think favours are peculiar to one nation and exclude others, plainly supposes a darkness in the understanding. For as God's love is universal, so where the mind is sufficiently influenced by it, it begets a likeness of itself and the heart is enlarged towards all men. (John Woolman)

Intercessions

We are called to be instruments of peace. With our service of the Gospel needing to be grounded in quiet prayer, we bring our needs to God, as we pray: *Keep us mindful of your love.*

- For all Christians, that our discipleship may be marked by a spirit of authentic prayer and a commitment to peace, let us pray . . .
- For all peoples, that governments and leaders may commit themselves to end every form of discrimination and intolerance, let us pray . . .
- For the Society of Friends—the Quakers—in thanksgiving for their profound gifts of quiet prayer, peacemaking, and service for the building up of the whole Body of Christ, let us pray . . .
- For those who suffer intolerance and persecution, that the spirit of William Penn, John Woolman, and their followers may give them hope in their struggles, let us pray . . .

Closing

Repeat morning's closing.

More on John Woolman
Woolman, John. *The Journal of John Woolman, and a Plea for the Poor.* New York: Corinth Books, 1961.

Catherine McAuley and Frances Xavier Warde

Founders and Missioners of the House of Mercy

*God raised up Catherine McAuley (1787–1841) to initiate
a religious movement in Ireland that evolved into the religious order of the Sisters of Mercy, who are dedicated to the
social and educational needs of the sick and the poor, especially poor women. Catherine was at the forefront of adapting
religious life for a society swiftly entering into the modern
age. Her colleague and close friend, Frances Xavier Warde
(1810–1884), took the new community to the United States,
where it became a rich blessing for the nation. In an age
when industrialization was accompanied by the problems of
poverty and illiteracy, both these women prophetically called
Christians to a new commitment to the spiritual and corporal
works of mercy. Their witness continues to call the church to
adapt the message of the Gospel for new times and new needs.*

MORNING

Call to Prayer

As with every day, God calls us to new pathways of service so that the mercy of the Gospel may feed every
person in need. This day we pray that God will open
our mind and heart to the divine will and make our
hands courageous so that we can feed poor people, bring
healing love to the sick, and assist all those in need that
we meet.

Fountain of all mercy,
your love is everlasting and without bounds.
Always you hear the cries of the poor.
Jesus, your beloved, moved among us
and brought your healing presence to all in need.
As this day dawns, we cherish the gift of your love
that provides for our needs
and bids us mercifully to serve one another.
In the welcome of this day,
we welcome one another.
We tend those our world forgets
and see in them the vision of your glory.

Praise

Catherine McAuley's world did not differ greatly
from our own. She found ways to be courteous to
poor people and her coworkers, and she encouraged
simple living. She fostered a welcoming spirit within
her works of mercy. In naming her first foundation
the House of Mercy, she identified a fundamental
value in her spirituality and in Christian living:
hospitality. Indeed, all Christian homes should be
houses of merciful hospitality. (Helen Marie Burns
and Sheila Carney)

Reading

In every age God raises up those who move us to greater
deeds of love and service. Grateful at this morning hour
for the life and witness of Catherine McAuley, Frances
Xavier Warde, and the Sisters of Mercy, we are called as
well to serve the lowly and forgotten. In joy we pray:
Honor, love, and praise be yours!

Acclamations

- We adore you, God, who never abandons the poor
  and the lowly, as we pray . . .
- We worship you, God, who calls each of us to serve
  those who are most forgotten, as we pray . . .
- We are filled with a spirit of gratitude for the many
  ways God's goodness is given to us when we suffer, as
  we pray . . .
- We give praise to you, God, who always hears the cries
  of the lonely and the dispossessed, as we pray . . .

Closing

God of mercy, you raised up your servants Catherine and Frances to bring the message of your goodness to the poor and the lowly, and to teach Christians everywhere to serve you in the forgotten. Never allow us to be deaf to the cries of those in need. Strengthen our hands in the spirit of their example that we may be instruments of your goodness to all we meet. We ask this as all things through Jesus our Messiah forever and ever. Amen.

EVENING

Call to Prayer

Daylight is fading, but the lamp of justice burns brightly in our midst. The example of the saints encourages us through the night until the dawning of God's everlasting day. With Catherine McAuley and Frances Xavier Warde, we keep faithful vigil for the final day of God's justice, peace, and mercy.

Thanksgiving

All praise and thanks to you, eternal God,
for your great, endless love.
You have never abandoned your people.
In Christ, you stand faithfully present to our needs
and to the sufferings of all the world.
In the spirit of Catherine McAuley and Frances Xavier
      Warde,
the spirit of Jesus was kindled in our midst
and the message of your mercy was heard anew.
All thanks be to you, eternal God,
for their faith and service
that move us always to greater love
of those whose lives are touched by sorrow.

Reading

As it is impossible to love God without manifesting a love for our neighbor, so it is equally impossible to love our neighbor without exhibiting it to him in our conduct, for . . . we show our feelings by acts.

. . . We must have a warm, cordial affection for all and manifest it by words, action and manner. In find, our charity must be in our hearts and from our hearts, and a charity such as Jesus Christ practiced while on earth. (Catherine McAuley)

We are always made bold by the living example of the saints. Grateful for the witness of Catherine McAuley and Frances Xavier Warde, who gave new richness to the virtue of mercy, let us offer our needs to our merciful God, as we pray: *Keep us mindful of your love.*

* For all Christians throughout the world, that we may be led by the Holy Spirit to serve those less fortunate than ourselves in love and not in pity, let us pray . . .
* For the Sisters of Mercy throughout the world and for all those who serve the poorest of the poor, let us pray . . .
* For those whose heart has been hardened and whose ears no longer hear the cries of the poor, that God may touch them gently in the spirit of new life, let us pray . . .
* For every public official, that the divine virtues of compassion, mercy, and love may be at the foundation of every decision and action, let us pray . . .

Repeat morning's closing.

Intercessions

Closing

More on Catherine McAuley

Bolster, Angela. *Catherine McAuley: Venerable for Mercy.* Dublin, Ireland: Dominican Publications, 1990.

Burns, Helen Marie, and Sheila Carney. *Praying with Catherine McAuley.* Winona, MN: Saint Mary's Press, 1996.

Cornelia Connelly

Educator and Worker
for Women's Dignity

Cornelia Connelly's life (1809–1879) was a living parable of Christ's death and Resurrection. She endured death among her children, abandonment by a husband who impulsively sought careers in both the Anglican and Roman clergies, and harassment as her husband tried to have her rejected from the convent life she later found was God's will for her. In an era when most societies refused to educate women, she founded the Sisters of the Holy Child Jesus for the betterment of women. Cornelia is today one of countless prayerful prophets whose legacy continue in her religious family's ongoing education of, and ministry to, children and women.

MORNING

Call to Prayer

At dawn the spirit of God hovers above our world breathing new life into our midst. As women and men created equally to steward creation, we join with Cornelia Connelly and all who champion human rights to work for the fullness of God's Reign.

Praise

O living God,
you fashioned our human race in your image
to be a community of equality and love among women
    and men.
With Cornelia Connelly and all the saints,
we worship you for binding us together in the love of
    Christ
to work tirelessly for the rights of every woman and
    man,
to tend creation as equal partners in holiness.

108

Your Spirit makes us one and calls us
to the task of Christian service,
so that the talents and gifts of every person
give glory to your holy name.

Reading

The Saints tell us many things which we take hold of and apply to ourselves only when the Holy Spirit gives us light to see, and the humility necessary to acknowledge when we do really see, and the fidelity to practise what He shows us. . . . It does happen that some think very little about the particular devotion to the Spirit from Whom all good comes. Now I wish for you all the Seven Gifts of the Holy Ghost, and that the Holy Spirit may whisper into your ear all that He wishes you to do. (Cornelia Connelly)

Acclamations

A new day has come. With the coming of the light, we are caught up in the anticipation of God's gift of equality for all peoples. In joy we pray: *Honor, love, and praise be yours!*

- We adore you, God, who called women and men to be equal stewards of all creation, as we pray . . .
- We are filled with joy for the love of God that breaks the bondage of discrimination and fear, as we pray . . .
- We worship you, God, whose Word made flesh has revealed the dignity of our human nature, as we pray . . .
- We are filled with hope for the presence of Jesus, who urges us to preserve the human rights of the poor and the oppressed, as we pray . . .

Closing

O God, from the womb of your goodness we have been brought to birth. With Cornelia Connelly and all women of faith, you urge disciples of Jesus to work tirelessly for the rights of every human being. Send forth your Spirit. Break the bonds of oppression and make us instruments of your justice and peace. We ask this as all things through Jesus our Messiah forever and ever. Amen.

EVENING

Call to Prayer

On this day God has called us to teach one another new pathways of peace. With Cornelia Connelly and all those who suffered for the education and dignity of the oppressed, we pray this night that we might teach others the freedom of life that comes to us in the presence of Christ Jesus whose word is life itself.

Thanksgiving

Tender teacher whose word is life,
you instruct the human heart
by the power of the Holy Spirit
to put aside the weaponry of human hate
and take up the staff of peace and justice.
Jesus, your beloved and holy child,
ever present in our midst,
joyfully leads us through the night
toward a new dawn of justice and peace.
This night we praise and thank you, O God,
for the gift of your holy ones,
who are mother and father for us,
teaching us your ways of liberty and holiness of life.
With them we proclaim you as our God
and the sole cause of our joy.

Reading

Do not allow your heart to be wounded, and if it is wounded in spite of your efforts, stitch up the wound with the love of God. . . . I very often have to remember this and . . . not to allow one's poor heart to drop blood till it withers! . . . He condescends to show us the love of His Heart, pointing to it and saying: "Learn of Me, for I am meek and humble of heart." (Cornelia Connelly)

Intercessions

With Cornelia Connelly and all those who work for the dignity of every woman, man, and child, we join our prayers to the God who wills justice for our life, as we pray: *Keep us mindful of your love.*

Catherine   Frederic   Cornelia

- For the church throughout the world, that the Christian community may teach others as Jesus did, let us pray . . .
- For universities, colleges, and schools, that they may be communities of humane and just learning while pursuing the life of the intellect, let us pray . . .
- For those who are called to the ministry of education, that the Spirit of wisdom may give them patience and joy as they labor to teach the Gospel, let us pray . . .
- For those who are held in the ignorance and fear that perpetuates human bondage, that God might set them free, let us pray . . .

Repeat morning's closing.

Closing

More on Cornelia Connelly

Flaxman, Radegunde. *A Woman Styled Bold: The Life of Cornelia Connelly*. London: Darton, Longman, and Todd, 1991.

Frédéric Ozanam

Husband, Father, Minister of Christian Charity for the Poor

Despite the upheavals of the French Revolution, a huge gulf between rich and poor people still existed in nineteenth-century France. The church had a resurgence, but deep suspicions toward it remained. This situation challenged Frédéric Ozanam (1813–1853), and he responded creatively. As a professor at the University of Paris, he showed how the church had served and should defend poor people, and how it had contributed steadily to human progress. He modeled what it means to be a loving husband and father. Perhaps he is best known now for founding the Saint Vincent de Paul Society, whose members worldwide still care for the material and spiritual welfare of impoverished people. Ozanam integrated devout faith, a towering intellect, a loving soul, and active charity; this is why he is considered holy and someone to be imitated.

MORNING

Call to Prayer

The rising sun shines on the rich and the poor alike. The spirit of God reminds us daily of our responsibility to care for the poor and those less fortunate because they are the special presence of God in our midst. With Frédéric Ozanam and all the saints, we pray that our service to the poor may be a generous sharing of ourselves, completely stripped of selfishness and condescension.

Praise

Merciful God,
from you comes the true wealth of the heart
and the spirit of generosity.

From of old you reminded your faithful people
that your presence is most clearly seen
in the poor and the disadvantaged.
As Jesus raised the poor,
we celebrate the life and ministry of your servant
  Frédéric Ozanam.
In his spirit we rejoice that you call us each day
to shed the light of human kindness and love
on those who cry for bread, for mercy,
and for that dignity of life that is at the heart of the
  Gospel.

Reading

Philanthropy is a vain woman for whom good actions are a piece of jewelry and who loves to look at herself in the mirror. Charity is a tender mother who keeps her eyes fixed on the infant she carries at her breast, who no longer thinks of herself, and who forgets her beauty for her love. (Frédéric Ozanam)

Acclamations

Each day God calls us to share with the poor our abundance and love without counting the cost to ourselves and without regard to our pride. In joy we pray: *Honor, love, and praise be yours!*

- We adore you, God, whose presence is found most graciously in the poor, the lowly, and the have-nots, as we pray . . .
- We are filled with wonder for the power of Christ in our midst that raises us to love the unfortunate, as we pray . . .
- We worship you, God, whose peace must be heralded by our deeds of justice in this world, as we pray . . .
- We are filled with love for your compassion, God, that never abandons the poor but hungers and thirsts with them, as we pray . . .

Closing

Loving God, in the presence of the poor, your love is made supremely manifest. Jesus commanded us to feed the hungry and give dignity to those upon whom the forces of evil have trodden. In the spirit of Frédéric Ozanam, send forth your Spirit. Dispel our fear and

quiet our timid heart. Move us to share our abundance
with the poor. Do not allow us simply to pity the less
fortunate, but to worship your presence in their midst.
Amen.

EVENING

Call to Prayer

In the growing darkness, we hear poor people cry out to
God and us for bread, for shelter, for kindness, and for
their promised share of the dignity of being human.
With Frédéric Ozanam and all the saints, we pray that
God would grant to the Christian community, to every
nation, and to every human heart, the gift of greater
generosity for the poor, until the forces of poverty are no
more.

Thanksgiving

O God, you love the poor and the dispossessed.
When you sent your beloved among us,
Jesus came not into the world of the powerful,
but into the impoverished streets and hearts of his time.
This night your Spirit moves among us once again.
We feel the power of Christ in our midst.
We hear his call to us to feed the poor,
to clothe the naked, to love the unloved.
And our selfishness and sin humbles us.
This night we offer you our repentant prayer of thanks,
knowing that the light of Christ in our midst
is leading us to a new day of Gospel compassion
wherein our heart can be made to overflow in love
for those who hunger for bread, for love, and for dignity.

Reading

The poor . . . are there and we can put finger
and hand in their wounds . . . ; and at this point
incredulity no longer has place and we should fall at
their feet and say with the Apostle, *Tu est Dominus
et Deus meus*. You are our masters, and we will be
your servants. You are for us the sacred images of
that God whom we do not see, and not knowing
how to love Him otherwise shall we not love Him in
your persons? (Frédéric Ozanam)

The poor and the lowly are the intimate friends of God. In the spirit of Frédéric Ozanam, we offer our needs this night, asking in a special way for the spirit of God to make us generous servants of the poor, as we pray: *Keep us mindful of your love.*

- For the church, that we might be divested of every sinful preference we may have for domination, privilege, prestige, and wealth, let us pray . . .
- For the nations of the world, that every law and structure of society may be founded on mercy and unselfish concern for the betterment of others, let us pray . . .
- For the members of the Saint Vincent de Paul Society, that their generous service of the poor may be blessed and may be an inspiration to all disciples of Jesus, let us pray . . .
- For the poor and disadvantaged people, that we may come to love them as Jesus loves us, let us pray . . .

Repeat morning's closing.

More on Frédéric Ozanam

Derum, James Patrick. *Apostle in a Top Hat.* Saint Louis, MO: Society of Saint Vincent de Paul, 1995.

Ramson, Ronald. *Praying with Frédéric Ozanam.* Winona, MN: Saint Mary's Press, 1998.

John Nepomucene Neumann
Bishop of Philadelphia

An immigrant from Bohemia and a priest of the Redemptorist religious community, John Neumann (1811–1860) was the fourth bishop of Philadelphia. The local clergy and social elite received "the Little Bishop," as he came to be called, with scant enthusiasm and eventual resentment, partly because of his focus on poor people and new immigrants. Before becoming bishop, Neumann had served in rugged American rural areas and city slums as a home missionary among the poor. As bishop, he initiated the free Catholic school system in Philadelphia and founded the Sisters of Saint Francis of Philadelphia for the promotion of education and health care. His sanctity was grounded in the quiet humility of a disciple of Jesus who dedicated his entire life to poor and lowly people for whom he made enormous personal sacrifices. Ultimately he was known and is venerated today as a man who did ordinary things extraordinarily well.

MORNING

Call to Prayer

In the morning breeze, we hear the ordinary sounds of life. Yet among the stirrings of this new day the graces of God are inviting us to the Gospel and to the service of all in need. With John Neumann and all the saints, we pray that the Spirit may open our senses to the cries of the poor and all those who are hungry for the Gospel of life.

God of all goodness and love,
in the simple beauty of field and flower
your grandeur and care are revealed.
Not to the powerful do you give glory,
but to the simple heart of those who believe.
Jesus walked among your poor,
declaring that theirs is the life of your Reign.
This day, with John Neumann and all the saints,
we give you praise and glory
for the gifts of your life,
which are seen in the striking eloquence
of human simplicity and love.

Praise

From your mother's womb, in the simplicity of your creation, I have knit together your bones and fashioned your soul in secret. I have known you and loved you from the moment of your creation. Do not believe that you are too small or too young. I will place my word within you that you might bear witness to my name before the powerful and the lowly alike. You are the messenger of my word to all the nations. (Jeremiah 1:4–10)

Reading

The grandeur of God is not found in things of power. God's grandeur is found in the ordinary simplicity of creation and life. In joy we pray: *Honor, love, and praise be yours!*

Acclamations

- We adore you, God, who makes known the message of the Gospel in the simplicity of creation, as we pray . . .

- We are filled with wonder for the power of the Word of life revealed in the faces of the poor and the lowly, as we pray . . .

- We worship you, God, who called John Neumann to tend the needs of the underprivileged and the poor, as we pray . . .

- We are filled with joy for your will, O God, that calls us this day and always to serve those who are most needy, as we pray . . .

Closing

O God, for the good of your people, you raise up shepherds whose ministry in the church is to be fashioned after the example of the poor Christ. In the spirit of John Neumann, teach us and all the ministers of your church to avoid every vestige of selfish pride and greed and to find your extraordinary honors in the ordinary service of those in need. Amen.

EVENING

Call to Prayer

As the world's daily work comes to a slow halt, we gather in this moment of prayer in praise and thanksgiving for the gifts of the day. We gather in repentance for the ways we have failed as disciples of Jesus. With John Neumann and all the saints, we pray this night that the light of Christ may strengthen us to take up the cross and celebrate the Resurrection.

Thanksgiving

God, source of every blessing,
to continue the work of the Gospel
you raise up in your church
shepherds and ministers in the image of Jesus
who tend your holy people
that we might be fashioned always into the Body of
     Christ.
We give you praise and thanks
for the life and ministry of John Neumann,
who stands as a shining example for every minister
of the selfless love of Christ,
the necessary foundation of all service.
This night we give you praise for such courageous
     witness
that refines and strengthens the mettle of our service
and moves us in the power of the Spirit
to be faithful servants of your Word and not our own.

Reading

Nothing would make me happier than an out-of-the-way little diocese where I would know my flock and call my priests by name. All my years as a diocesan priest in western New York, as a Redemptorist missionary . . . fifteen of them—have been training for just such a diocese as "Pottsville." I have the background and the character for such a place. I'm long hardened to travel by horsecart and canal barge. All my life I've liked walking. I have hiked over mountains and down long valleys from one settlement to the next preaching the word of God. (John Neumann)

Intercessions

We are the Body of Christ. We offer our needs to God in the hope that our life in Christ for the service of the world will be renewed, as we pray: *Keep us mindful of your love.*

- For the church, that the hallmark of our life as the Body of Christ will be the loving care of those who are underprivileged and poor, let us pray . . .
- For clergy and all church ministers, that the Spirit will lead them away from greed, selfishness, and that greatest of lusts, that is, the adoration of power, let us pray . . .
- For all who serve the poor, that the spirit of God will be their strength when they encounter hardships and fatigue, let us pray . . .
- For the church, that our Christian life may enrich and challenge our nation for an authentic and loving welcome of the tired, the poor, and the wandering, let us pray . . .

Closing

Repeat morning's closing.

More on John Neumann
Galvin, James J. *Blessed John Neumann.* Baltimore, MD: Helicon, 1964.

Harriet Tubman
Escaped Slave, Abolitionist, Witness for Freedom

Harriet Tubman (c. 1820–1913) escaped from slavery in Maryland and defied the laws by working with the Underground Railroad to liberate more than three hundred slaves. Such courage sprang from a deep faith in Christ Jesus, whose death and rising freed all humanity from the slavery of sin. Tubman's work and her example are indicative of the prophetic lengths to which true believers will go in putting flesh on their baptism into Christ.

MORNING

Call to Prayer

As the sunlight advances across our life, we are reminded of the periods of history when the powerful enslaved other human beings in the name of commerce and cultural domination. The Gospel of Christ stands in opposition to every form of slavery. This day we pray with Harriet Tubman that the power of the Spirit will lead us to work tirelessly for the liberation of every woman, man, and child who is still bound by the many forms of slavery's chains.

Praise

Liberator of the human family,
this day we give you praise and adoration
for the brilliant Son of justice,
whose Resurrection has rescued all of creation
from the dark forces of power and domination.
This day we recognize those places of our world
and those crevices of the human heart
that have refused the light of your freedom.

This day we celebrate the power of Christ among us
who can lead us to work for the shattering of the chains
that keep your people in bondage and pain.
This day our heart rejoices that we can be your
    messengers,
grown strong in the Holy Spirit,
to lend our hands and heart to your victory.

Reading

Israel has passed through the sea of slavery and has
set foot on the dry land of freedom. The prophet
Miriam takes up her tambourine and dances with
wild abandon in the seawind gusts that gale over the
defeated forces of Pharaoh. "O Israel, sing to the
Holy One with wild abandon. Sing to the one who
has raised us up. This is the day of God's victory—
shattering the forces of slavery and setting our
people free." (Exodus 15:20–21)

Acclamations

God has broken the chains of slavery, and the Spirit
spreads the winds of freedom across the face of the
earth. In joy we pray: *Honor, love, and praise be yours!*
• We adore you, God, who did not abandon us but gave
  us a final victory in the Resurrection of Christ, as we
  pray . . .
• We are filled with wonder for the power of Christ
  that bids us to continue to work for the freedom of
  those still in chains, as we pray . . .
• We worship you, God, who calls every believer to the
  tasks of justice, freedom, and peace, as we pray . . .
• We are filled with joy for the evidence of Christ's
  victory each time that our heart resists the power of
  domination and greed, as we pray . . .

Closing

God of joy, when your people cried out to you from the
slavery of Egypt, you did not abandon them but deliv-
ered them to the Promised Land of freedom. In the final
victory of Christ in the Resurrection, our freedom from
the power of the evil one was fulfilled. Praying with
Harriet Tubman and those who have struggled for
liberation in every age, send forth the power of your

Spirit and break the chains that bind your children.
Bring us all to the Promised Land that we might sing
forever of your victory in Jesus. Amen.

EVENING

Call to Prayer

Gathered in from the growing darkness, we are warmed
and enlightened by the light of Jesus, who is forever the
victorious one who has rescued us from the power of
evil. With Harriet Tubman and all those who witnessed
against slavery, we pray this night that God's freedom
may come to all those whose lives are still held in chains
and bondage of any form.

Thanksgiving

Loving and gracious God,
from the beginning you created us in freedom
and you sealed that gift
through the Resurrection of Christ.
This night we give you praise and thanks.
We confess to you, O loving God,
our slowness to set the captives free
by disarming our heart of hatred's power.

Your Spirit calls us into a new light
and asks that we surrender our life to you
and place our hands on the plough of human freedom,
working for that day when every chain will be broken
and every captive will be free.
With Harriet Tubman,
we celebrate our salvation in Christ,
who is the fountain of life
for the freedom of the whole world.

> There was one of two things I had a *right* to, liberty, or death; if I could not have one, I would have the other; for no man should take me alive; I should fight for my liberty as long as my strength lasted, and when the time came for me to go, the Lord would let them take me. (Harriet Tubman)

Reading

With Harriet Tubman, we celebrate the God who desires the freedom of every human being. In the spirit of human liberation, we offer the needs of the world to God, as we pray: *Keep us mindful of your love.*

Intercessions

- For the church, that our commitment to human life will include our every effort to resist the evils of racism and slavery, let us pray . . .
- For all the nations, that human governments will never again permit the horror of human slavery, let us pray . . .
- For those who continue to enslave others by their senseless bigotry and racial hatreds, that they be brought to conversion, let us pray . . .
- For those who still suffer in the chains of every form of human bondage, that they may come to freedom and peace, let us pray . . .

Repeat morning's closing.

Closing

More on Harriet Tubman
Bradford, Sarah Elizabeth. *Harriet Tubman, the Moses of Her People*. New York: Corinth Books, 1961.

Sojourner Truth
Prophet of Women's Rights and Racial Equality

Many Christian saints and heroes led a hard life and told tough truths, making other people and themselves uncomfortable. Sojourner Truth (c. 1797–1883), born a slave with the name Isabella Baumfree, gained her freedom and spent the rest of her life struggling to free slaves and liberate other women. Motivated by deep Christian convictions, Sojourner Truth confronted people with their racism, sexism, fears, and selfishness. Her legacy is a sharp reminder to each of us that a commitment to Christ is a commitment to work for the freedom of every human being regardless of the price to oneself or others.

MORNING

Call to Prayer

The light of this new day opens our eyes to the immense price demanded of living the Gospel. Deep within our heart, we know that our love of Christ requires that we enter into a manner of living that cannot be easy. We pray this day with Sojourner Truth that the Spirit will give us the strength and faith for active love, ready to confront the forces of slavery and evil in our world in the name of Jesus.

Praise

God of life and freedom,
in the beginning you created us in equality
and gave us to one another in love and mutual care.
Yet, in the course of human history,
greed and selfishness overtook us.
We enslaved one another in hate and violence.

124

Your Spirit moves among us this day,
urging us in imitation of Jesus
to wrestle with the forces of evil
that keep your children in chains.
With Sojourner Truth and every freedom fighter,
you make us strong to resist evil
and to build for you a world that sets the captives free.

Reading

That little man in black there [a preacher], he says women can't have as much rights as men, 'cause Christ wasn't a woman! Where did your Christ come from? Where did your Christ come from? From God and a woman! Man had nothing to do with Him.

If the first woman God ever made was strong enough to turn the world upside down all alone, these women together ought to be able to turn it back, and get it right side up again! And now they is asking to do it, the men better let them. (Sojourner Truth)

Acclamations

At this dawning, God opens our ears to hear the voices of those who are crying for freedom. We are committed in the spirit of Sojourner Truth to work for human freedom in the name of Jesus. In joy we pray: *Honor, love, and praise be yours!*

- We adore you, God, whose desire is for the equality of women and men, of all the races, of all people, as we pray . . .
- We are filled with gratitude for the strength of the Spirit that makes us bold to work for the liberation of all our sisters and brothers, as we pray . . .
- We worship you, God, who raised up Sojourner Truth to sting the conscience of the churches and our society, as we pray . . .
- We are filled with wonder for each time that the spirit of God disarms the human heart of hatred and bigotry, as we pray . . .

Closing

O God, your daughter Sojourner Truth strode in strength and Gospel beauty to tell us in her prophetic voice of the horror of slavery and the sinful inconsistency of the unequal treatment of earth's daughters. Rouse your Spirit and make us disciples of Jesus working for human freedom. Fill us with the presence of Jesus to set your people free. We ask this as all things through Jesus our Messiah forever and ever. Amen.

EVENING

Call to Prayer

As evening comes again, our heart is painfully aware of the terrors of the night that visit the life of the world's enslaved even in their waking hours. The Gospel is not a message of convenience. This night we pray for the power of Jesus to make us strong workers for the end of oppression and the dawn of a true justice that sets all the captives free.

Thanksgiving

God of compassion,
you stand close to your people in their suffering,
and you comfort those who are afflicted.
You never abandon us to the dark powers of evil,
but have given us the light of Jesus
by which to find our way to freedom's path.
In every age you raise up prophets and teachers
who continue to lead us in the spirit of Christ,
that we might enter into the mighty struggle
for the victory of human freedom over slavery.
With Sojourner Truth and all your saints,
we give you praise and thanks for your gifts.
We confess that we are
too often slow to stir against oppression and fear.
Your Spirit glows among us,
giving us your strength
that we might announce
that you are a God
who loves mercy, justice, and liberty.

Reading

Look at my arm! I have ploughed and planted, and gathered into barns, and no man could head me! And ain't I a woman? I could work as much and eat as much as a man—when I could get it—and bear the lash as well! And ain't I a woman? I have borne thirteen children, and seen them most all sold off to slavery, and when I cried out with my mother's grief, none but Jesus heard me! And ain't I a woman? (Sojourner Truth)

Intercessions

Our world is still filled with human bigotry based on race, color, creed, gender, sexual orientation, and ethnic origin. We are confident that God will hear our prayer that we might break the chains of human oppression, as we pray: *Keep us mindful of your love.*

- For the church, that we might be made courageous to confront the evils of oppression, let us pray . . .
- For the nations, that the evils of hatred, discrimination, and inequality may be ended in our time, let us pray . . .
- For every human heart, that the Spirit might turn us from fear and hatred to open our hands in love toward all human beings, let us pray . . .
- For all those who are the victims of violence, hatred, and oppression, that the Spirit may salve their wounds and rouse us to their liberation, let us pray . . .

Closing

Repeat morning's closing.

More on Sojourner Truth
Painter, Nell Irvin. *Sojourner Truth: A Life, A Symbol.* New York: W. W. Norton, 1996.

Susan B. Anthony

Abolitionist,
Pioneer for Women's Suffrage

Susan B. Anthony (1820–1906) blended deep Christian faith with a lifelong career of social action. She was the daughter of a Quaker father who gave her educational experiences that blossomed into her efforts to abolish slavery, to advocate temperance on behalf of abused wives and children, and to fight for the rights of women. She never lived to see the day when her struggle for suffrage led to changes in the law. However, Anthony is honored as one of the legendary figures associated with civil rights for women, minorities, and the suffering. Her radical witness is a testimony to the strength of the Holy Spirit born out of the profound depth of quiet prayer intrinsic to the Quaker tradition of Christian faith.

MORNING

Call to Prayer

At the start of this day, we remember the life and work of Susan B. Anthony, who worked tirelessly and selflessly for the freedom of women, minorities, and those who suffered abuse. In her, the Holy Spirit gives us the witness of consistency between the words of faith and faith's action. We pray this day that God will bless us with the same strength of Gospel life and conviction.

Praise

Loving God,
we give you praise and worship
for the Gospel of Jesus Christ that is our life.
Jesus walked among us to teach us how to live.
He sealed his teachings and his mission
with his life-giving death on the cross
and then his glorious, hope-filled Resurrection.

In every age you raise up women and men
who point the way to Christ's life
by their putting into action
the words that their lips profess.
This day, with Susan B. Anthony,
we honor and celebrate your life within us,
acknowledging that your Holy Spirit, the spirit of truth,
provides us with the strength and courage
to continue to put our flesh on your word.

Reading

The woman of the future will far surpass her of the present, even as the man of the future will surpass him of to-day. The ages are progressive. . . . I think this is to be obtained somewhat by making the sexes coequal. When women associate with men in serious matters, as they do now in frivolous society ones, both will grow better and the world's work will be better done than it is now. I look for the day when . . . the only criterion of excellence or position shall be the ability, honor, and character of the individual without regard to whether he or she be male or female. And this time will come. (Susan B. Anthony)

Acclamations

On this new day, God calls us to live the Gospel with the works of our hands and not simply the words of our lips. In joy we pray: *Honor, love, and praise be yours!*

- We adore you, God, who created women and men as equal stewards of the beauty of creation, as we pray . . .

- We are filled with gratitude for the life of tireless workers whose efforts advance the cause of God's justice and peace in society, as we pray . . .
- We worship you, God, who led Susan B. Anthony to preach the Gospel in her efforts for those made victims by the self-hatred of others, as we pray . . .
- We are filled with wonder for the power of the Holy Spirit, who fashions the strength of heaven's mercy in the quiet of simple prayer, as we pray . . .

Closing

God of justice and mercy, we are grateful for the life and witness of Susan B. Anthony, who followed Jesus to the cross and continued Jesus' ministry by working for the freedom of slaves, the equality of women, and the healing of innocent victims of addiction. In that same Spirit, raise us up to be apostles of your justice in the hope of your everlasting peace. We ask this as all things through Jesus our Messiah forever and ever. Amen.

EVENING

Call to Prayer

As the shades of evening fall, the lamp of Christ's justice burns brightly in our midst. Gathered from the streets, we bear with us to our home the memories of those whose lives cry out to know the meaning of that justice. In the example of Susan B. Anthony, we pray this night that God will give us the strength to live out the message of Christ by our work on behalf of justice and equality in the world and in the church.

Thanksgiving

Loving and gracious God,
we give you praise and thanks this night.
You are the fountain of mercy
and the foundation of all justice.
We celebrate this night the Resurrection of Christ
that is the light of salvation never fading.
Yet in our world, the forces of inequity and pain
still hold hostage many fearful hearts.
In every age you raise up women and men of courage
who hear the word and put it into practice.
In the spirit of these courageous witnesses,
your Spirit moves among us this night
inspiring us to open our heart fully
that the words of our faith
may be given testimony in deeds of justice.

Reading

I pray every single second of my life; not on my knees but with my work. My prayer is to lift women to equality with men. Work and worship are one with me. I know there is no God of the universe made happy by my getting down on my knees and calling him "great." (Susan B. Anthony)

Intercessions

Our world still hungers for the fullness of God's justice and peace. Confident that the night will give way to the dawn of God's Reign, we bear our needs to God, as we pray: *Keep us mindful of your love.*

- For the church, that the people of God may bring our faith in Christ to fruition by our labors for equality and justice, let us pray . . .
- For the nations, that the scandals of inequality, oppression, and domination may be rooted out from human society, let us pray . . .
- For those who are still deprived of their equal rights or equal protection under the law, that God might move us to help them know freedom and peace, let us pray . . .
- For those who have been victimized and abused by the disease of addiction, that God might bring them consolation and comfort as their loved ones come to healing, let us pray . . .

Closing

Repeat morning's closing.

More on Susan B. Anthony

Sherr, Lynn. *Failure Is Impossible: Susan B. Anthony in Her Own Words.* New York: Random House, 1995.

Thérèse of Lisieux
The Little Flower
of the Little Way

*The wisdom of the Gospel calls for witnesses to the gift of
simplicity. Thérèse of Lisieux (1873–1897), known as the
Little Flower, is one of the saints whose only extraordinary
mark on life was her ordinariness. Indeed, had it not been
for the publication of her autobiography and the account
of miracles after her death, she may have passed through
history largely unnoticed. Her legacy to Christian spirituality
is the unquestioned and radically important truth that the
ordinariness of human life offered to God is the most fitting
vessel for the extraordinary gift of God's grace. This spirituality of simplicity has come to be known as the Little Way.*

MORNING

Call to Prayer

We open our eyes and heart to the breaking of a new
day. Called from sleep, we prepare to enter our world,
with its tasks and challenges. Called to discipleship in
Christ, we ask God to mark our ordinary daily tasks with
the extraordinary gift of Christ's presence for the good of
our sisters and brothers and for the glory of God.

Praise

Good and loving God,
your goodness is our sole glory.
You do not desire great deeds of heroism
such as the world would judge greatness.
Rather, you ask only the offering of our simple faith
and the free gift of our love,
that in our life and service
you might be glorified with all the ordinary elegance
of the field lily and the sparrow's song.

With the Little Flower and all the saints,
we adore your presence this day
and give you praise for your love,
which graces our life with the only dignity
that causes our soul to sing and dance.

> But this love of mine, how to shew it? Love needs to be proved by action. Well, even a child can scatter flowers, to scent the throne-room with their fragrance; even a little child can sing, in its shrill treble, the great canticle of Love. That shall be my life, to scatter flowers—to miss no single opportunity of making some small sacrifice, here by a smiling look, there by a kindly word, always doing the tiniest things right, and doing it for love. (Thérèse of Lisieux)

Reading

With the Little Flower and all the saints, we acclaim the God of all goodness whose glory is fully manifest in the simplicity of our life and all creation. In joy we pray: *Honor, love, and praise be yours!*

Acclamations

- We give praise to you, God, whose life is found in the beauty of creation, as we pray . . .
- We are filled with joy by you, God, who does not ask us for greatness, but only for our love and devotion, as we pray . . .
- We adore you, God, who never abandons us in our weakness but guides our every breath and movement, as we pray . . .
- We are filled with love at your presence, God, who calls us to the gentle service of one another and all the world, as we pray . . .

Loving God, with all the eloquence of our ordinary life, your goodness is sung. You completely revealed your love when Jesus took on the simplicity of human existence. With the Little Flower and all the saints, teach us to serve you in our daily life, seeking not worldly greatness but the grandeur that is the life of the Gospel. We ask this as all things through Jesus our Messiah forever and ever. Amen.

Closing

EVENING

Call to Prayer

As this day comes to an end, we lift our soul in gratitude to the God who has opened us to grace in the midst of our every daily endeavor. Joyful for the Christ who enlightens our life this night and always, we join with the Little Flower and all the saints to sing of God's goodness that is ever kindled in our midst.

Thanksgiving

Loving and gracious God,
with believers of every time and place,
we acclaim that the simplicity of the Gospel
is your gift to us, enamored as we are
with vanity and passing pride.
Your goodness and favor may be manifested
in deeds of power and acclaim.
But more often your mercy comes
through ordinary acts of human love and tender care.
Jesus, our beloved savior,
make known your presence in our simple flesh.
The divine wounds of Christ,
manifest in the life of the Little Flower,
press on us as well and mark our life with your love.
This night and forever we are yours,
and our simple song of thanksgiving wells up within us
to every land and nation
that is in need of your truth and freedom.

Reading

What an extraordinary thing it is, the efficiency of prayer! . . . I just do what children have to do; . . . I tell God what I want quite simply, without any splendid turns of phrase, and somehow he always manages to understand me. For me, prayer means launching out of the heart towards God; . . . it's a vast, supernatural force which opens out my heart, and binds me close to Jesus. (Thérèse of Lisieux)

With Thérèse of Lisieux, the Little Flower, and all the saints we offer our needs to the God who asks of us nothing more than the simple offering of our undivided heart, as we pray: *Keep us mindful of your love.*

- For all Christians, that we might find in the Little Flower a fitting image of the simplicity of prayer and service to others, let us pray . . .
- For all those who are searching to become poor in spirit in imitation of the Beatitudes, let us pray . . .
- For missionaries to whom the Little Flower is a special companion and a gifted witness of Christian prayer and ministry, let us pray . . .
- For those whose life is encumbered with the temptation of ungodly pride and obsession with worldly greatness, let us pray . . .

Repeat morning's closing.

More on Thérèse of Lisieux

Clarke, John, trans. *Story of a Soul: The Autobiography of Saint Thérèse of Lisieux.* Washington, DC: ICS Publications, 1975.

Schmidt, Joseph F. *Praying with Thérèse of Lisieux.* Winona, MN: Saint Mary's Press, 1992.

Frances Xavier Cabrini

Minister to Italian American Immigrants, Courageous Spirit

*Foreign immigrants to the United States oftentimes meet
fear and economic deprivation. Frances Xavier Cabrini
(1850–1917), known as Mother Cabrini, was instrumental
in the foundation of an innovative religious community of
women designed to meet the educational and social needs of
Italian immigrants. Her initial ideas met with disapproval,
but over the course of thirty-five years, she founded nearly
seventy institutions to serve poor people, orphans, the uneducated, and the sick. She traveled all over the United
States and to Central and South America, serving God's
people. Her innovative spirit testifies to the powerful grace
of the Spirit if one is open to a life that is truly Gospel-worthy.*

MORNING

Call to Prayer

At the beginning of this new day, God opens before us
an invitation to act from our faith in ways unexpected.
We pray for the strength of the Holy Spirit in our life to
follow God's paths despite our human reluctance, fear,
and lack of insight. We ask God to make us courageous
to follow the Gospel path.

Praise

God of every blessing,
we see the splendors of your love dawn upon us
through the rich diversity of the human family.
How abundant, how deep, how unfathomable
is the mystery of your love in the varieties of cultures.
Into the Americas you brought the gifts of many peoples,
that from the many you might create one family

to offer the image of true liberty and freedom to all the
world.
This day, with Mother Cabrini as our companion in the
faith,
we celebrate the presence of your Spirit,
who invites us always and in every place
to welcome all those who search for your beauty and
peace,
or who seek the opportunity to live with hope and
dignity.

How can we put a limit to our affection and to our
energy when we consider the interests of Jesus? . . .
    Let us not shirk and dream and wait to help His
children who are this moment in pain, in want,
crushed and abandoned by the society of men who
are mortal microscopic things compared to Christ!
Let our . . . hands do the work of a hundred hands
and bring His love and aid to the lost souls, to the
poor in prisons, tenements, streets, mines, hospitals,
fields and wherever is suffering! (Frances Xavier
Cabrini)

Reading

With Mother Cabrini and all who work for people in
need, we celebrate the love of God that knows no
distinctions or divisions. In joy we pray: *Honor, love,
and praise be yours!*

Acclamations

- We offer you, God, our adoration for the diversity
of the peoples of every nation and culture, as we
pray . . .
- We are filled with wonder at the power of the Holy
Spirit, who inspires us to equity and just treatment of
our sisters and brothers, as we pray . . .
- We offer you, God, the worship of our life as we are
filled with gratitude for your grace that is our salvation, as we pray . . .
- We are filled with love for your compassion and
grace, God, that urges us to the service of the poor, as
we pray . . .

Closing   O God, you raised up Mother Cabrini to serve the needs of poor and uneducated immigrants. By her example and the power of your Spirit, do not let us shrink from your command to welcome the wandering, the tired, and the lonely into our heart and life. Amen.

EVENING

Call to Prayer   This night we celebrate the wonder of the Gospel that is not bound by human fear. The lamp of Christ enlightens our mind and heart, as it did Mother Cabrini, to spread the Word of life to those who are threatened by the shade of ignorance and hatred. We pray that the Spirit may light our way into the presence of the poor people who so desperately need our love and assistance.

Thanksgiving   O God, desire of every heart,
we give you praise and thanksgiving
for the wonders of your love
reflected in the diverse richness of the nations.
You called our ancestors to service and care
of those who were wandering and poor
because they are the reflection of your holy presence.
This night we pray in the spirit of Mother Cabrini,
who followed the command of Jesus
to bring the Good News of salvation
to every human being without distinction.
This night your Spirit stirs us
to go forth in a new Pentecost of generosity
to meet the needs of the wandering poor
and to bind all hearts into your one family.

Reading   God alone has put into the mind of [humans] the divine spark of intelligence. The poet, the states-man, the artist, the scientist, all owe to God the genius that makes them outstanding, and the Church, amongst the titles she gives to the Holy Ghost, calls Him the Spirit of Wisdom and Intellect. It is meet, therefore, that we should draw water from the source, and so, after having worked on our part and studied assiduously, we must have recourse to Our Lord and expect from Him memory, intelligence and success. . . . Pray . . . but not at length, for with all the work we have to do, you have little time and must pray briefly but with fervor. (Frances Xavier Cabrini)

The gift of salvation and the gifts of the Spirit are offered to every person without distinction. In that spirit we offer our prayers to God for the spread of the Gospel and the wisdom of the Spirit among every nation and people, as we pray: *Keep us mindful of your love.*

Intercessions

- For the church universal, that we may be open to the spirit of adaptation for the preaching of the Gospel in every land, let us pray . . .
- For Christian leaders, that the Spirit may give them the courage to move us to a greater generosity for poor people and the lonely, let us pray . . .
- For all the nations, that the Spirit may remove the sins of human hatred, bigotry, and violence from our midst, let us pray . . .
- For those who must make their home in new lands, that they may know the gift of consolation and comfort in their trials, let us pray . . .

Repeat morning's closing.

Closing

More on Frances Xavier Cabrini
Sullivan, Mary Louise. *Mother Cabrini: Italian Immigrant of the Century.* New York: Center for Migration Studies, 1992.

Bill W. and Dr. Bob

Founders of Alcoholics Anonymous

Bill W. (d. 1971) and Dr. Bob (d. 1950) brought the blessings of Alcoholics Anonymous (AA) to millions of women and men. Based on a rigorous program of honesty and complete surrender into the hands of a loving higher power, Alcoholics Anonymous has helped people become more conscious of the disease of addiction. Bill W. and Dr. Bob were instrumental in providing a living witness to the power of spiritual recovery to those who society had counted as morally weak and hopelessly lost. Today the legacy of Bill W. and Dr. Bob continues to offer a spiritual way of living for all those, Christian or not, who seek a daily reprieve from the ravages of addiction.

MORNING

Call to Prayer

As daylight enters into our life, we invite to consciousness the God of our understanding, who enlightens our way and bids us cast off every power of darkness that holds us prisoner to fear and hopelessness. With all those who are searching for a daily reprieve from the disease of addiction, we join with Dr. Bob and Bill W. to proclaim that God has indeed broken every yoke and shown us a pathway to genuine freedom and happiness.

Praise

Source of all goodness and life,
you have made us in your image to give you praise and
    glory.
From your grace, the gift of our salvation in Christ,
so many have stumbled and fallen ill
by the alluring destruction of addiction and despair.

Yet you do not leave us alone and without aid, O God.
You offer grace and healing to all those who fall ill;
you give the courage to rise up anew,
to grasp your strong, helping hand,
and to move straight forward with a heart deeply healed.
This day and forever you are the God who travels our
    pathways
and never leaves us to be victims of sickness and despair.

God, I offer myself to Thee—to build with me and **Reading**
to do with me as Thou wilt. Relieve me of the bondage to self, that I may better do Thy will. Take
away my difficulties, that victory over them may
bear witness to those I would help of Thy Power,
Thy Love, and Thy Way of Life. May I do Thy will
always! (*Alcoholics Anonymous*)

We are conscious that the power of God has broken **Acclamations**
every form of human bondage and offers the endless
possibilities of peace and health to us. In joy we pray:
Honor, love, and praise be yours!
- We adore you, God, who has willed us to be at peace
  with ourselves and with all the world, as we pray . . .
- We are grateful for the presence of you, God, who
  alone is the health for every human ill, as we pray . . .
- We honor you, God, whose graces are made manifest
  each day in the life of those who have embraced recovery, as we pray . . .
- We are filled with joy at the power of God's love in
  the life of those who are addicted or those who serve
  those afflicted with addiction, as we pray . . .

O God, you who always seek out the lost and the **Closing**
wounded, you raised up your servants Bill W. and Dr.
Bob to witness in their lives and service the power of
your healing for those in search of recovery. Stretch
forth your hand upon those in the bondage of disease
and despair. Breathe forth new life into the wounded.
Bind us in love for the service of one another until that
day when your victory shall bring a final end to every

oppression of body and spirit. We ask this as all things
through Jesus our Messiah forever and ever. Amen.

EVENING

Call to Prayer

Darkness falls. Seeing the shade cross the streets and
into our life, our thoughts turn to those whose lives have
been darkened by fear and trembling. This night we
remember especially those who suffer from the disease of
addiction. With them, we pray in the spirit of Bill W.
and Dr. Bob that the God of our understanding will aid
us with the power of the Holy Spirit to surrender our
every need before the One who alone can heal our every
wound.

Thanksgiving

O God, when Jesus stretched his arms on the cross,
he gathered all things of this earth up into your presence.
Even in his agony in the garden,
Jesus surrendered himself into the fullness of your care.
You know us well, O God.
We cannot hide from your truth.
You see how often we turn from you
and seek destructive pleasures
that can never bring us eternal life.
Yet you do not leave us to our own devices
or to the changing appetites of our heart.
You call us constantly back to Christ.
You are the God whose victory alone brings us health.
You are the God whose love alone can bring us happiness,
You are the God whose life alone is the full measure of
     peace.
All praise and thanks to you, eternal God of life
for the gift of salvation and health you give
to all those whose lives are marred by sadness and despair.

Reading

Everything we do involves some kind of dedication.
When we simply try to reform a troublesome
addiction, our struggle is dedicated to minimizing
the pain that addiction causes us and others. But in
consecration we dedicate our struggle to something

more; consecration is our assent to God's transform-
ing grace, our commitment homeward. (Gerald May)

Intercessions

The reality of suffering brings us to the power of prayer.
With all those in recovery, grateful for that extraordinary grace, we bring our needs before the God of all
healing, as we pray: *Keep us mindful of your love.*
- For all Christians, that in our mutual care for one
  another we may proclaim the gift of God's healing, let
  us pray . . .
- For all those in recovery, that their experience, hope,
  and strength may be a gift of joy to others, let us pray
  . . .
- For all women and men who assist those touched by
  the disease of addiction, that their courageous service
  may move us to a greater love of those in need, let us
  pray . . .
- For all those who wander still in any form of addiction and bondage, let us pray . . .

Closing

Repeat morning's closing.

More on Alcoholics Anonymous
Alcoholics Anonymous. New York: Alcoholics Anonymous World Services, 1976.

John XXIII
Pastoral Pope for the Modern Age

*When John XXIII, born Angelo Giuseppe Roncalli
(1881–1963), was elected pope in 1958, few observers
expected any great accomplishments from this jolly, kindly,
portly pope. So, most everyone was surprised when he con-
voked the Second Vatican Council. He saw clearly that the
church was no longer a European institution, but a worldwide community made up of diverse cultures, values, gifts,
and needs. The church also needed to respond to develop-
ments in technology, politics, economics, and science. Mostly
John wanted to see the church serve the people of God.
Although John XXIII died in 1963, two years before the
Council ended, his inspiration, goodness, and Gospel vision
guided the church to open dialog with believers of other
denominations, to renew liturgical practice, and to commit
itself to social justice and peacemaking.*

MORNING

Call to Prayer

At the breaking of the day, the word of God once again
draws us to give flesh to the Gospel in fresh ways. With
John XXIII and all the saints, we pray this day that the
Spirit may give us the courage to preach the word of
God passionately, tenderly, courageously, and lovingly.

Praise

Loving God,
you gave to our first parents
the garden of your delights as their home.
You dwelled among us and celebrated our joy
as beloved of your creation.
Even when we sinned, you loved us.

In time you sent us the greatest gift of your love,
the Messiah, the Christ,
who gave us the gift of salvation.
With John XXIII and all people of goodwill,
we praise and adore you for the gifts of creation,
in which you bid us live in the fullness of your grace.
This day and forever you shepherd us in peace,
that we might be the instruments of your love
for all the ages and nations of the world.

Reading

Any human society, if it is to be well ordered and productive, must lay down as a foundation this principle, namely, that every human being is a person, that is, his nature is endowed with intelligence and free will. By virtue of this, he has rights and duties of his own, flowing directly and simultaneously from his very nature, which are therefore universal, inviolable, and inalienable. (Pope John XXIII)

Acclamations

On this day of the new creation we give praise to God, who calls us to preach the Good News in diverse and marvelous ways. In joy we pray: *Honor, love, and praise be yours!*
- We adore you, God, whose word of life is ever ancient and yet ever new, as we pray . . .
- We are filled with love for you, our Creator, who shepherds through ministers and friends attentive to the needs of the human heart and spirit, as we pray . . .
- We worship you, God, who raised up John XXIII for the reform and renewal of the church and the building of the people of God, as we pray . . .
- We are filled with happiness and peace at the revelation of God, who teaches us in Jesus the joys of living, as we pray . . .

Closing

Shepherd of souls, with John XXIII we celebrate your love in our life. Send us the power of your Spirit that we might prefer your love before all else. Teach us to seek out the wounded heart and bring the gift of healing to a world that hungers for your justice. Inspire us to open the doors of your house of prayer to all those who long to dance again to the strains of your passionate love. Amen.

EVENING

Call to Prayer

As the day comes to an end, we celebrate the light of Christ that can never be extinguished. The Gospel burns brightly in our midst to lead us into a final era of everlasting peace and justice. With John XXIII and all the saints, we pray for the universal church that God's people may be faithful in proclaiming God's constant faithfulness and mercy.

Thanksgiving

God of brilliant truth and kindness,
Jesus brings light to our soul,
dispels the power of evil,
and leads us in a pilgrimage of faith.
This night we give you praise and thanks.
We offer you the incense of our repentant prayers.
Your Spirit burns within our heart
and makes us hunger for your goodness,
that we might give the gifts you have given us
as bread and drink for the life of the world.
With John XXIII and kindly pastors of every age,
we celebrate your goodness,
which alone can satisfy
the cravings for truth of the human heart.

Reading

The Church has always had the duty of scrutinizing the signs of the times and of interpreting them in the light of the Gospel. Thus, in language intelligible to each generation, [the Church] can respond to the perennial questions which [people] ask about this present life and the life to come, and about the relationship of the one to the other. (*The Pastoral Constitution on the Church in the Modern World*)

In joyful memory of the life and courageous witness of John XXIII, we ask God for a new outpouring of the Spirit, as we pray: *Keep us mindful of your love.*

Intercessions

- For the church, that the spirit of God may be poured out on us in a new Pentecost of unity, peace, and love, let us pray . . .
- For the church's pastors, that they may be filled with a spirit of concern that moves them to prefer the human heart to sterile precepts, let us pray . . .
- For those who wander searching for the truth that can satisfy their mind and heart, let us pray . . .
- For all those who resist the promptings of the Spirit experienced in the signs of the times, that Christ might enlighten them and grant them the strength to encounter God's presence in this world, let us pray . . .

Repeat morning's closing.

Closing

More on Pope John XXIII
John XXIII. *Journal of a Soul.* New York: McGraw Hill, 1965.

Thomas Merton

Contemplative, Activist, Trappist Monk

Thomas Merton (1915–1968) stood at the heart of a wide-spread resurgence of interest in spirituality in the 1950s. Merton's book The Seven Storey Mountain *recounts his early life, his dramatic conversion after his college years, which he describes as filled with confusion and aimlessness, and his first days as a Trappist. To the surprise of most people, this spiritual memoir proved enormously popular and launched his ministry as a spiritual writer. His works found their center in his lifelong struggle with conversion into the person of Jesus. His story and insights of faith have become vital spiritual nourishment for untold numbers of people all over the world. Merton, long involved in dialog between Christianity and other world religions, met an untimely death while attending an East-West religious conference in Bangkok, Thailand, in 1968. His spiritual legacy continues to provide enrichment for all who are looking to find a lively life of prayer and a solid grounding for Christian activism in the world.*

MORNING

Call to Prayer

Like the certainty of the rising sun, God is always faithful. This day God calls us as a faith-filled people to prayer and to action. With these two responsibilities as its hinges, we open the door to this new day and ask for the gift of the Holy Spirit to make us faithful in seeking Christ in prayer and seeking our sisters and brothers in the loving that is Christian service.

Faithful God, your warmth spreads across us at this new day and bids us to prayer before your glory. You are the blazing forth of love itself that takes away our breath and brings us to loving silence. Your Spirit moves within us at this new day and gives us words that can only be spoken in the intimacy of the heart. From the heart of this world, we give you adoration and praise as the cause of our joy and the center of the whole universe. Praise to you, O God of silence and words!	**Praise**

The Lord plays and diverts Himself in the garden
of His creation, and if we could let go of our own
obsession with what we think is the meaning of it
all, we might be able to hear His call and follow Him
in His mysterious, cosmic dance. . . . We are invited to forget ourselves on purpose, cast our awful
solemnity to the winds and join in the general dance.
(Thomas Merton)

Reading

From the silence of our heart, our faith cries out with
deafening praise of the God who has called us to the
grace of loving. In joy we pray: *Honor, love, and praise be
yours!*

Acclamations

- We adore you, God, who draws us more deeply into
  the heart of silence, as we pray . . .
- We are filled with wonder at you, God, whose divine
  will is made manifest clearly in the silent mists of
  morning, as we pray . . .
- We honor you, God, who is always with us as our life
  is deepened in the spirit of conversion into Jesus, as
  we pray . . .
- We are filled with joy for the spirit of prayer that calls
  us to the service of all our sisters and brothers, as we
  pray . . .

Closing | O God, whose voice is heard in silence, we give you thanks and praise for the life and ministry of Thomas Merton. As you called him into the heart of Christ through prayer and ministry, call us to yourself that our life of prayer and our service of one another may be enriched and made bold by the power of your Holy Spirit. We ask this as all things through Jesus our Messiah forever and ever. Amen.

EVENING

Call to Prayer | As the shadows extend into our world, we are called to sense what deeds of mercy we have done for God on this day. In the spirit of Thomas Merton, we realize that the life of faith is not an escape from the world. Prayer urges us into the heart of the world itself, into the life of those who are needy. We ask for the grace of the Holy Spirit to open our heart that we might be made bolder for deeds of justice when a new day dawns.

Thanksgiving | God of the evening rest,
at this day's end you call us to surrender our life
into your loving spirit of revelation.
At prayer we open our heart to you
to look deeply into our life and loving.
Your Spirit, who calls us from the silence of prayer
into the life of the world itself,
moves us in generosity to share the gifts you have given
    to us
with those who are likewise hungry for your presence
in our deeds of justice, mercy, and peace.
This night and forever you blaze forth
with the light of life, our savior Jesus Christ,
that we might extend your warmth and love
to all those who are in need.

Reading | Christian social action is first of all action that discovers religion in politics, religion in work, religion in social programs for better wages, Social Security, etc., not at all to "win the worker for the Church," but because God became man, because every man is potentially Christ, because Christ is our brother, and because we have no right to let our brother live in want, or in degradation, or in any form of squalor whether physical or spiritual. (Thomas Merton)

Our life in God is forever joined to our service of needy and poor people. Realizing that a faith without loving service to others is no faith at all, we offer our needs to God, as we pray: *Keep us mindful of your love.*

Intercessions

- For all Christians, that our life of prayer may move us to greater deeds of justice, mercy, compassion, and peace, let us pray . . .
- For an end to that spirit that tempts us to forget that the life of prayer must overflow into the service to others, let us pray . . .
- For all contemplatives, in gratitude for their faithful witness of prayer and concern that leads us to a greater examination of the depth of our life in Christ, let us pray . . .
- For those who run from the invitation of God to a life of prayer and Christian service, let us pray . . .

Repeat morning's closing.

Closing

More on Thomas Merton

Merton, Thomas. *The Seven Storey Mountain.* New York: Harcourt Brace Jovanovich, 1948.

Shannon, William. *Silent Lamp: The Thomas Merton Story.* New York: Crossroad Publishing Company, 1992.

Simsic, Wayne. *Praying with Thomas Merton.* Winona, MN: Saint Mary's Press, 1994.

Dietrich Bonhoeffer

Lutheran Pastor,
Resister Against Nazism, Martyr

*The life, work, martyrdom, and writings of Dietrich Bon-
hoeffer (1906–1945) have become a focal point in the study
of Christian spirituality. A Lutheran pastor, Bonhoeffer
participated in an assassination plot against Adolf Hitler.
Bonhoeffer escaped to England but came to believe that his
underground activities were cheapened in the face of his
escape. His return to Germany cost him his life, but it gave
to him the graced belief that his life was crowned by accept-
ing the full price of a Gospel stance against the horrors of the
Holocaust and the nightmare of the Nazi regime. Grace does
not come cheap.*

MORNING

Call to Prayer

Another day of grace has come upon us. This day the
spirit of God calls us to deeds of justice and mercy. In
the spirit of Dietrich Bonhoeffer we open our ears to
hear the cries of those in our world who have been victimized by the forces of evil. We pray this day for the
grace of Christ to make us strong to work tirelessly on
behalf of the freedom of those who are oppressed and
made to suffer.

Praise

Loving God,
you sent your beloved Jesus into our midst
to walk among us and declare your year of favor.
The powers of his age raged against him
and eventually killed him,
thinking that this would silence him, your Word.

But from that horrible death,
you made that wood a tree of life.
Salvation flowed from the Resurrection of the crucified
    Jesus
to bring hope to captives, healing to the wounded,
and liberation to those who are in chains.
With Dietrich Bonhoeffer and every martyr,
we give you praise and adoration for the gift of the Spirit,
who emboldens us through grace
to fight the good fight
until that day when your promise of freedom shall be
    fulfilled.

Reading

Christ exists among us as community, as Church in the hiddenness of history. The Church is the hidden Christ among us. . . . Man can no longer understand himself, but only from Christ. (Dietrich Bonhoeffer)

Acclamations

With martyrs, we give God praise for the gift of salvation that liberates human hearts. In joy we pray: *Honor, love, and praise be yours!*

- We adore you, God, who desires that chains be broken and that freedom reign in every nation, as we pray . . .
- We are filled with joy for the courage of the martyrs that instills in us the power to resist evil and proclaim the victory of the cross and Resurrection, as we pray . . .
- We worship you, God, whose grace was the passion of Dietrich Bonhoeffer's life and ministry, as we pray . . .
- We are filled with love for the power of Christ who calls us, like Bonhoeffer, to work for human dignity and justice, as we pray . . .

Closing

Loving God of all creation, when dark forces in history raised up the specter of evil and oppression to enslave your Chosen People and those whom society regarded as outcasts, you raised up your servant Dietrich Bonhoeffer with women and men of faith to give their lives freely so as to bring to an end the horrors of war and hatred. Stir your Spirit within us that we may, in our own ways, surrender to the cost of the Gospel of Christ and continue to work for the gifts of freedom and peace that flow from Jesus. We ask this as all things through Jesus our Messiah forever and ever. Amen.

EVENING

Call to Prayer

Night has come again. In the growing darkness we sense the presence of hatred, bigotry, oppression, and discrimination—forces that seek to erode the dignity of human life. In the darkness, God lights the lamp of Christ to bring us hope and to warm our soul so that we might resist evil and proclaim the victory of the Resurrection. With Dietrich Bonhoeffer and all martyrs for human freedom, we pray this night that we might be instruments of peace for all those who suffer.

Thanksgiving

All powerful God,
you do not abandon your people in troubled times,
but promise to be with us until the dawn.
As Jesus gave his life for us upon the cross,
and then triumphed over death in the Resurrection,
so we acknowledge in praise and thanksgiving
those who have followed in discipleship
and have given their lives for the freedom of the world.
Your Spirit moves among us
to calm our timid and frightened heart.
Your Spirit makes us bold to confront the forces of evil
and resist those who would rob the children of earth
of the dignity with which you have blessed us.

Reading

Grace is *costly* because it calls us to follow, and it is *grace* because it calls us to follow *Jesus Christ*. It is costly because it costs a [person] his [or her] life, and it is grace because it gives a [person] the only true life. (Dietrich Bonhoeffer)

In the death and Resurrection of Christ, God has vanquished the powers of evil. With Dietrich Bonhoeffer and every martyr, we present the needs of the world, that the grace of freedom may continue to take root in history, as we pray: *Keep us mindful of your love.*

- For the church, that the witness of the martyrs may make us strong to struggle for the freedom of every people, let us pray . . .
- For all nations, that our Christian witness may herald that day when the power of oppression shall be broken forever, let us pray . . .
- For those who are called to the ministries of justice and peace, that the spirit of God may console them in troubled times, let us pray . . .
- For the great cloud of witnesses, especially for those like Dietrich Bonhoeffer who have given their life as a witness against evil and oppression, let us pray . . .

Repeat morning's closing.

More on Dietrich Bonhoeffer

Bonhoeffer, Dietrich. *Letters and Papers from Prison.* New York: Macmillan, 1971.

Dag Hammarskjöld
Pioneering Leader
for World Peace

Some believe that war is an inevitable part of the human condition. Many more prefer to believe that world peace is a dream attainable in reality if only we would grasp it. Dag Hammarskjöld (1905–1961), Secretary General of the United Nations in the 1950s, was one of those who preferred to dream about and work for world peace. He was an intellectual and a man of poetic depth. His writings reveal someone who was deeply aware of the human condition and of our human possibilities in grace. His life and his tragic death while on a mission of peace in Africa in 1961 remind every believer in Jesus that all Christians should be peacemakers.

MORNING

Call to Prayer

Daylight pours again into our world with the bright promise of new challenges of faith. As the day dawns, the spirit of God inspires us to deeds of peace and justice. We pray this day that the Spirit may make us pioneers for peace, first by disarming our own heart of hatred, fear, and enmity.

Praise

O God, you set our heart on peace.
Be praised above the nations, O God of glory,
for you do not leave us to our own devices,
but you raise up in our midst
prophets and leaders
who turn our thoughts away from enmity
and call us to be people of your peace.

This day we give you praise for the life and witness
of Dag Hammarskjöld and world leaders
whose hearts yearn for an end to war,
an end to every form of hatred,
and the dawning of your eternal peace and justice.

Reading

I don't know Who—or what—put the question, I
don't know when it was put. I don't even remember
answering. But at some moment I did answer *Yes* to
Someone—or Something—and from that hour I
was certain that existence is meaningful and that,
therefore, my life, in self-surrender, had a goal. (Dag
Hammarskjöld)

Acclamations

At this dawning, with Dag Hammarskjöld and leaders
who move us to justice, we are filled with a hunger for
God's peace in the world. In joy we pray: *Honor, praise,
and might be yours!*
- We adore you, God, whose peace is planted deep in
  our heart and in our desires, as we pray . . .
- We are filled with joy for the witness of courageous
  leaders who call us to deeds of justice and peace, as
  we pray . . .
- We worship you, God, who will not abandon our
  world to the dark forces of fear, war, and destruction,
  as we pray . . .
- We are filled with wonder for the signs in our world
  of a new thirst for Christ's peace as the cornerstone of
  human living, as we pray . . .

Closing

God of all love, you made us in peace yet our hands too
often grasp for the machinery of war. You do not abandon us to our sinful ways, but you raise up prophets and
leaders who call us back to your goodness. With Dag
Hammarskjöld and all those who work for peace, teach
us to cast off the weaponry of hatred. Move us to open
our arms to raise up all in this world toward the vision of
your love and peace. Amen.

EVENING

Call to Prayer   As our daily labors come to an end, the Spirit of Jesus in our midst moves us to reflect upon what we have done for God this day. Confident that our Creator will bind up our sinfulness and renew us in sleep to take up the labors of peace once again, we offer this evening thanks, asking only that God's peace might flower in our time.

Thanksgiving   O God, you whose peace is bread for our hunger,
you are the object of our desire
and the fullness of the promise of justice.
In the fullness of time,
you sent Jesus into our midst
that he might reveal your justice in our flesh.
With leaders like Dag Hammarskjöld,
your Spirit burns in our midst
and enlightens our pathways,
so that we might put aside the weaponry of war
and walk forever in your peace,
upholding in dignity those who are frail and weak.
With the lamp of Christ's peace burning in our midst,
we give you praise and thanks forever.
Your justice and mercy are without end.

Reading   In a dream I walked with God through the deep places of creation; past walls that receded and gates that opened, through hall after hall of silence, darkness and refreshment—the dwelling place of souls acquainted with light and warmth—until, around me, was an infinity into which we all flowed together and lived anew, like the rings made by raindrops falling upon wide expanses of calm dark waters. (Dag Hammarskjöld)

Intercessions   We are grateful for the life and witness of leaders like Dag Hammarskjöld who work in myriad ways for the fullness of world peace. We are confident that God will fulfill Christ's peace in our midst, as we pray: *Keep us mindful of your love.*

- For all disciples of Jesus, that we may be built up as a community of faith serving as instruments of peace in the world, let us pray . . .
- For governments and nations, that the justice and peace of God's Reign may be the foundation of every constitution, let us pray . . .
- For all world leaders, that they may teach the nations to put aside greed, war, and oppression and take up the cause of the oppressed, let us pray . . .
- For all in our world whose lives are ravaged by war and oppression, that our efforts may be the sign of the Spirit's liberation in their lives, let us pray . . .

Repeat morning's closing.

Closing

More on Dag Hammarskjöld

Hammarskjöld, Dag. *Markings*. New York: Alfred A. Knopf, 1964.

Stolpe, Sven. *Dag Hammarskjöld: A Spiritual Portrait*. New York: Scribner, 1966.

Van Dusen, Henry P. *Dag Hammarskjöld: The Statesman and His Faith*. New York: Harper and Row, 1967.

Martin Luther King Jr.
Martyr for Human and Civil Rights

Martin Luther King Jr.'s (1929–1968) faith led him to a course of public, nonviolent, civil protest against the forces of racial discrimination in the United States. His life and work, which ended in his martyrdom, have been a radical witness for subsequent generations who continue to labor for human and civil rights, for equal protection under the law, and for liberty, justice, and freedom on behalf of every human being who still suffers discrimination and injustice.

MORNING

Call to Prayer

Christ lives in our midst, and so we rise confident that in Christ our life can be made into an instrument of peace and justice. With Martin Luther King and all those who work for human rights, we pray that the spirit of God may make us courageous to take up the graces and crosses that are part of ridding ourselves of violence and discrimination, and that are part of allowing God to pour into our heart the oil of healing and justice.

Praise

Blessed and glorious are you,
O God of all creation,
for the bright dawn of salvation
that has broken into our life.
In the beginning you fashioned us in love
and bid us love one another with the same tender care
with which you brought us to creation.
Despite the ravages of hatred,
you raise up prophets and teachers
to speak your word of peace.

In the fullness of time, you sent to us our Christ
whose life was your presence in our midst.
Crucified for our sake, Christ is among us.
The Savior's word and power is echoed
by many servants such as our brother Martin.
All praise and glory be yours, O God of justice,
for you sustain us this day until that final dawn
when every chain of slavery will be broken
and all your children shall walk in unending freedom.

Reading

I will sing always to God the victorious one!
Horse and rider, God has thrown into the sea.
Our chains have been broken
and we walk dry-shod to the glory land.
Freedom rings for every heart.
Broken bones are mended.
Crooked limbs are straightened.
God has made salvation known,
and we walk now into freedom.

(Exodus 15:1–3)

Acclamations

We remember with joy the life and witness of our brother Martin Luther King Jr. Grateful for his life of service, we are refreshed to enter this day confident that God will give us the courage to give flesh to the Word of life. In joy we pray: *Honor, love, and praise be yours!*

- We glory in you, God of all creation, who has called the human race to live in dignity, freedom, and peace, as we pray . . .
- We give thanks and praise for the memory of Martin Luther King, and for all those who have given their life for justice and freedom, as we pray . . .
- We are filled with wonder at the power of the Word, for which women and men have sacrificed their life, as we pray . . .
- We are thankful for the memory of Martin Luther King, whose life of courage has given us hope that human equality is a dream coming to fruition, as we pray . . .

Closing

God of mercy, we honor the memory of Martin Luther King Jr., who gave his life that the hope of true liberty might burn ever brighter in this world. By the power of his example, strengthen us to work for justice and freedom for all your children. We ask this through the power of Jesus our Messiah forever and ever. Amen.

EVENING

Call to Prayer

Evening is swiftly coming upon us. Despite the advancing shadows, our heart is strengthened by the lamp of justice that burns brightly among us. This day we have celebrated the life and witness of Martin Luther King, whose courage and faith have been a living testimony to the power of God's truth that sets us free.

Thanksgiving

Author of all justice and peace,
when your people walked in darkness
you saw fit to send into our midst
a brilliant lamp that never dims,
a lamp that leads us in every age
into the bright promise of a day without end.
Jesus, your lamp of justice,
crucified upon the wood
of ignorance, fear, and hatred,
gave his life that we might live,
and showed us how to love one another.
This day we honor the memory of our brother
Martin Luther King Jr.,
so in love with our Savior
that he offered his life's blood
to be poured out as well
in love of justice and peace.
With Martin and with martyrs for peace in every age,
we give you praise and thanks
for the justice and peace of Jesus that are life.

Now that Christ has come, we have been justified under the grace of freedom. We are no longer subject to the discipline of the law. We are all God's children now without distinction. There is among us no longer male or female, slave or free, Jew or Gentile. Rather, we are all one because we belong to Christ and therefore to one another. (Galatians 3:23–29)

Reading

As we honor the life and memory of our brother Martin Luther King, let us offer our needs to God, as we pray: *Keep us mindful of your love.*

Intercessions

- For all of God's people, that our life of faith may overflow each day into words and deeds that set free all those who are held in bondage of any form, let us pray . . .
- For those who work for justice, peace, and equality for every woman, man, and child, that their life may be borne up in courage each time that they are made to suffer for their faith, let us pray . . .
- For each of us, that like Martin Luther King we may see the invitation to conversion and rid every form of prejudice from our heart and mind, let us pray . . .
- For all those who are the victims of prejudice, hatred, and fear, that the presence of Christ may console them, let us pray . . .

Repeat morning's closing.

Closing

More on Martin Luther King Jr.
Washington, James Melvin, ed. A *Testament of Hope: The Essential Writings of Martin Luther King Jr.* San Francisco: Harper and Row, 1986.

Maximilian Kolbe and Oscar Romero

Martyrs for the Ransom of the Many

One of the most moving images of our crucified Savior is as the man who gave his life for ransoming the world. Maximilian Kolbe (1894–1941) took this image seriously and literally. During World War II, this Polish Franciscan exchanged his life for that of a young, married man who was to be executed in reprisal for another prisoner escaping from a Nazi concentration camp. He ransomed the life of an oppressed and persecuted man, and was himself martyred. Oscar Romero (1917–1980), the courageous El Salvadoran archbishop, took seriously the preferential option for the poor of his native church. Romero, without regard for his own safety, spoke out time and again against the social injustices perpetrated upon the people. He was gunned down in 1980. He too gave his life as a ransom in Christ, believing passionately that the church does not detach us from the world but immerses us in it. He was murdered for his love of Christ that drew him to serve the liberation of the poor in his country.

MORNING

Call to Prayer

At the beginning of this day, we remember Christ's abiding presence and the renewed gift of salvation that was won for us at the sacrifice of the cross and then through the glorious Resurrection. We pray this day with Maximilian Kolbe, Oscar Romero, and the martyrs for justice in every age, that all disciples of Jesus might give themselves selflessly so that the lives of all our sisters and brothers may be lived in Gospel peace.

Praise

God of all salvation,
this day we give you praise and worship
for the gift of your life that has set us free.
Your light of revelation has dawned upon us
with the gift of hope that is ours in the crucified and
   Risen Christ.
With Maximilian Kolbe, Oscar Romero, and all your
   martyrs,
we sing the praises of your Reign,
for which the poor and the oppressed still long.
Your Spirit rouses us from sleep
to put on the armor of faith today
so that the poor and the lowly will be defended.
You are the defender of the poor
and the crown of all those
who give their life for Christ Jesus,
for the ransom of many.

Reading

To combat evil . . . is to fight with love for all
. . . including those who are less good. It is to put
goodness in relief, so as to make it more attractive.
. . . When the occasion presents itself to call the
attention of society, or of authority, to some evil, it
must be done with love for the person to blame.
(Maximilian Kolbe)

Acclamations

As day begins, our mind turns to the vision of the Savior
who has ransomed us from death through his dying and
rising. In joy we pray: *Honor, love, and praise be yours!*
• We adore you, God, whose love has been victorious
  in the life-giving death and Resurrection of Christ, as
  we pray . . .
• We are filled with awe at the majesty of the cross and
  the glory of the Resurrection that have ransomed us
  from the power of evil, as we pray . . .
• We worship you, God, who gives strength to the
  martyrs as witnesses to unselfish love before all the
  ages, as we pray . . .
• We are filled with hope for that final day when the
  victory of Christ shall be fulfilled in the coming of
  God's Reign, as we pray . . .

Closing

Eternal and merciful God, in the cross and Resurrection of Jesus Christ, the power of the evil one has been broken, and our life has been ransomed from death. We pray with Maximilian Kolbe and Oscar Romero, who gave their lives for the ransom of the lowly, that your Holy Spirit may keep us hopeful and make us strong for the works of mercy and justice. By our fidelity to resisting the power of evil, may your Reign be heralded and may your world be renewed. We ask this as all things through Jesus our Messiah forever and ever. Amen.

EVENING

Call to Prayer

As darkness stills the earth, may the silence heighten our hearing of the cries of those who are threatened by the grim forces of evil and oppression. With the cross of Jesus and Christ's empty tomb before our eyes, we are strengthened by the example of ransoming love in the martyrdom of Maximilian Kolbe and Oscar Romero. With them as our companions, we pray for an end to the dark night of injustice and the coming dawn of God's peace.

Thanksgiving

Holy, mighty and immortal one,
the cross of Jesus and Christ's empty tomb
shine in the night as our flames of hope.
We give you praise and thanks
for Jesus, who offered his life
for the ransom of many.
With the cries of the oppressed in our ears,
our heart is made strong by the Spirit
to put on the armor of selfless love
and struggle for that day of mercy
when your justice and peace will reign supreme.
With Maximilian Kolbe, Oscar Romero, and all the
        martyrs,
your Spirit unites us as one community of faithful
        witnesses
to proclaim the message of the Gospel
in the face of oppression and evil.

Reading

"Whoever out of love for Christ gives himself to the service of others will live, like the grain of wheat that falls and only apparently dies. If it did not die it would remain alone. . . . Only in undoing itself does it produce the harvest." (Oscar Romero)

Intercessions

Christ gave his life as ransom that we might live. Hopeful of the final coming of peace and justice, we offer our needs to God, as we pray: *Keep us mindful of your love.*

- For the church, that our preaching of the Gospel will permit us to stand in solidarity with the oppressed, even to the point of suffering, let us pray . . .
- For missionaries, especially for those who risk their lives in love, that the Spirit may give them joy in their struggles and hope in the face of danger, let us pray . . .
- For the family of nations, that governments will surrender laws and practices that deny human rights and freedom, let us pray . . .
- For each of us, that the presence of Jesus in our life will teach us to surrender the armaments of hate and oppression that are the origins of all war and violence, let us pray . . .

Closing

Repeat morning's closing.

More on Maximilian Kolbe and Oscar Romero

Craig, Mary. *Six Modern Martyrs.* New York: Crossroad Publishing Company, 1985.

Hodgson, Irene, trans. *Archbishop Oscar Romero: A Shepherd's Diary.* Cincinnati, OH: Saint Anthony Messenger Press, 1993.

The Women Martyrs of El Salvador
Lives Given in Love

Lay missioner Jean Donovan, Maryknoll sisters Ita Ford
and Maura Clark, and Ursuline sister Dorothy Kazel—
the names of these women and their brutal martyrdom are
etched into the heart of believers. These missionaries in El
Salvador worked among the poorest of people, touching the
lives of the poor with the peace that can only spring from
faith in Jesus. For their efforts, they were raped and mur-
dered. The age of martyrs has not ended. These women lost
their lives because they sought, like Jesus, to heal, to teach
the Good News, and to free the captive. The forces of evil
cannot tolerate such goodness. As in the early church,
memory of these witnesses has stirred others to take their
place in the struggle for peace and justice.

MORNING

Call to Prayer

As the light of a new day enters our life, the spirit of
God calls us to spread the Gospel. Each day we realize
that our commitment in Christ demands that we set our
hands to the plow of justice until that final day when
the fullness of justice will flower. With Jean Donovan,
Dorothy Kazel, Maura Clark, and Ita Ford, we pray for
the coming of the day of peace that is heralded by our
works for justice in this time and in all places where
God's will takes us.

Foundation of every human hope,
in the original darkness of the abyss,
amid the pangs of your labor of love,
you gave birth to us in your image
to be a people of justice and peace.
This day, your brilliant Son of justice
spreads the light of the Gospel before our eyes,
that we might see again the wondrous vision of your
     love
and be moved in strength to deeds of mercy and
     compassion.
You open our heart to see your poor
and bid us open our hands to feed them
with bread and dignity.
This day you draw us to love you in the poorest of all
and to feed one another as you have fed us.

Praise

There's one thing I know, that I'm supposed to be
down here, right now. . . . You can contribute a lot
and make a big difference in the world if you realize
that the world you're talking about might be very
small—maybe one person, or two people. And . . .
if you can find a place to serve, you can be happy.
(Jean Donovan)

Reading

With love we call to mind the witness of martyrs of
every time and place. In the spirit of their generosity, we
grasp the challenge of Gospel living on this day. In joy
we pray: *Honor, love, and praise be yours!*
- We adore you, God, who has spread before us the
  Gospel feast of justice and peace for all people, as we
  pray . . .
- We are grateful for the vocation of mercy and compassion that is given to us in baptism, as we pray . . .
- We honor you, God, whose justice demands that we
  confront the forces of oppression and evil in every
  corner of human life, as we pray . . .
- We are filled with joy for the presence of the Spirit
  wisdom, in whose birthing we are made bold for the
  service of others, as we pray . . .

Acclamations

Closing | O God of justice, with Maura Clark, Ita Ford, Dorothy Kazel, and Jean Donovan we celebrate the message of the Gospel that sets free the captives of our world. Make us living witnesses to the freedom of Christ until that day when the blood of the martyrs will flower with the fullness of your peace. We ask this as all things through Jesus our Messiah forever and ever. Amen.

EVENING

Call to Prayer | As this day draws to a close, we join with the women martyrs of El Salvador to pray for the final scattering of the darkness of oppression in every corner of the world. In our midst is burning the lamp of justice, the living presence of Jesus Christ, who lights our pathways and leads us to serve only the Gospel of peace and justice. The light of Christ warms us with hope and strength to meet with hope the terrors of the night that threaten the poor and the lowly.

God of all compassion,
you walked in the garden
and sought out our parents even in their naked fear.
You never allow your people to be alone,
but stand close to us in the terrors of the night.
Jesus, your beloved, walked among us in our poverty,
embraced our fears,
and dispelled them in the glory of the Resurrection.
With the women martyrs of El Salvador,
and with your living witnesses,
Jesus continues to walk among us,
bringing the light of hope
where we are too often held in the darkness of oppression.
This night your Spirit moves among us once again
and beckons us deeper still to new deeds of justice and
    peace
until that final dawn,
when your truth and mercy shall bring to an end
all forms of despair and suffering.

Thanksgiving

Wherever the gift of healing and liberation in
however partial a manner reaches the winterized
or damaged earth, or peoples crushed by war and
injustice, or individual persons weary, harmed, sick,
or lost on life's journey, there the new creation in
the Spirit is happening. (Elizabeth Johnson)

Reading

God's heart always opens to the cries of the poor. Just as
Jesus walked among us to bring the mercy of God to the
lowly, so too do we offer our needs to God, as we pray:
Keep us mindful of your love.
- For all Christians, that our baptism into the ministry
  of Christ may consecrate us daily for the service of
  the poor, let us pray . . .
- For every nation, that governments and leaders may
  make the peace of the Gospel the foundation of every
  constitution, let us pray . . .
- For all those whose life of justice and peace is a living
  martyrdom for the raising up of the poor and the
  enslaved, let us pray . . .

Intercessions

- For the downtrodden and those who are oppressed, that the spirit of God and the work of our hands may set them free, let us pray . . .

Closing

Repeat morning's closing.

More on the Women Martyrs

Carrigan, Ana. *Salvador Witness: The Life and Calling of Jean Donovan*. New York: Simon and Schuster, 1984.

Zagano, Phyllis. *Ita Ford: Missionary Martyr*. New York: Paulist Press, 1996.

Dorothy Day
A Catholic Worker for Justice and Peace

Dorothy Day (1897–1980) confronted the conscience of Americans, especially Catholics, to see the radical implications of a Gospel commitment to justice and peace. After embracing Catholicism, Day founded the Catholic Worker Movement with Peter Maurin, and she started The Catholic Worker *newspaper, which was intended to comfort the afflicted and afflict the comfortable. She started the first House of Hospitality to offer food, clothing, and shelter to poor people. Day steadfastly opposed war through her nonviolent protests. Dorothy Day indeed gave new meaning to what it means to be holy: combining unity with the poor and service to them, struggling for justice, offering compassionate hospitality, integrating ministry and prayer. Her life is a living parable of active love and faith in Christ Jesus.*

MORNING

Call to Prayer

As daylight breaks, the truth of the Gospel again dispels the darkness of night. Each day God calls us to a deeper faith in Christ Jesus. Each day God asks that we give flesh again to the Word who is our life. This day we remember the life and work of Dorothy Day. We are moved by her prophetic sacrifices for the poor and the oppressed. With her we pray for the increased commitment to building God's Reign in our midst by our renewed deeds of justice and peace for those who have no advocates.

Praise

All honor and praise be yours,
almighty and ever living God.
Each day your Spirit rouses us from sleep
to put on the armor of light
and go forth to proclaim the truth of the Gospel
in deeds of mercy, justice, and peace.
As daylight breaks, you bid us give flesh
to the Word, who is our life and freedom.
With saints and ancients of every time and place,
you bid us preach the Gospel by our deeds of justice
and thereby be your instruments of peace
until the last darkness of human oppression has been
    dispelled.

Reading

An understanding of the dogma of the Mystical
Body is perhaps the greatest need of the present
time. It is a further explanation of the Incarna-
tion. . . .
    Christ is the head and we are the members. And
the illnesses of injustice, hate, disunion, race hatred,
prejudice, class war, selfishness, greed, nationalism,
and war weaken this Mystical Body, just as prayer
and sacrifices of countless of the faithful strengthen
it. . . .
    All men are our neighbors and Christ told us we
should love our neighbors, whether they be friend or
enemy. (Dorothy Day)

Acclamations

In celebration we call to mind the life and witness of
Dorothy Day who called the church of Christ to a new
dawning of peace and justice as the hallmark of a Gospel
life. With her and all the saints, we celebrate the price
of the Gospel in our life. In joy we pray: *Honor, love, and
praise, be yours!*
- We worship you, God, who created us for freedom
  and for loving, as we pray . . .
- We honor you, God, who opens our eyes to the needs
  of the poor and the oppressed, as we pray . . .

- We bless the presence of the Merciful One, who strengthens and empowers our hands for works of peace, as we pray . . .
- We are grateful for the presence of the Spirit, who enlivens us in hope until that day when the fullness of peace shall dawn, as we pray . . .

Closing

Gracious and merciful God, you do not wish your beloved children to wander in loneliness and pain. As Jesus did, you call us always to minister to those whose hunger and thirst for justice and peace are insatiable. With Dorothy Day and all the saints, strengthen our heart and hands for the service of the poor, until that day when the fullness of your justice and peace will flower. We ask this as all things through Jesus our Messiah forever and ever. Amen.

EVENING

Call to Prayer

With the coming of the night, we open ourself to the light of Christ heard in the cries of the poor. Millions wander in hopeless poverty and are tempted to despair.

For them Christ kindles a lamp in our midst to light our
way to love tenderly, act justly, and walk humbly. This
night we pray for and with Dorothy Day and all those
who work for justice and peace. With them we are joined
forever in the challenge of the Gospel to preach a year of
jubilee by liberating every prisoner of poverty and fear.

Thanksgiving

O God who moves with brilliant love
in the shades of the evening,
from the simple elegance of earth
you fashioned our heart for love and dignity.
From long ago you taught us
that you are most manifest
in the lives of the poor and those who need our love.
This night and forever,
with Dorothy Day and all people of justice,
you bid us go forth into the night
and search out those whose lives are seared
by the angry wounds of poverty and despair.
For them you ask us to light the lamp of justice
by feeding their needs and tending their wounds.
You are the strength that makes bold our hands
for the works of loving justice.
You are the comfort that tends our fears.
You are the brilliance that leads us on in hope
until the final coming of Christ's justice and peace.

Reading

It is no use saying that we are born two thousand
years too late to give room to Christ. . . . Christ is
always with us, always asking for room in our hearts.

But now it is with the voice of our contempo-
raries that He speaks, with the eyes of store clerks,
factory workers, and children that he gazes; with the
hands of office workers, slum dwellers, and suburban
housewives that He gives. . . . And giving shelter
or food to anyone who asks for it, or needs it, is giving it to Christ. (Dorothy Day)

We are grateful for the witness of heroic Christians who remind us that a commitment to the Gospel of Christ is a commitment to justice and peace. With Dorothy Day and all who minister to the poor, we offer our needs to God as we pray: *Keep us mindful of your love.*

- For all Christians, that the spirit of God may make us ever mindful of our call to serve the needs of all God's people, let us pray . . .
- For all those who have embraced a life of voluntary poverty so as to serve the needs of the poor and the lowly, let us pray . . .
- For all those whose lives prophetically challenge the spirit of complacency and selfishness in society, let us pray . . .
- For the poor and the dispossessed, for the fearful and the suffering, that our deeds of mercy may be their comfort, let us pray . . .

Repeat morning's closing.

Intercessions

Closing

More on Dorothy Day
Allaire, James, and Rosemary Broughton. *Praying with Dorothy Day.* Winona, MN: Saint Mary's Press, 1995.

Day, Dorothy. *The Long Loneliness: The Autobiography of Dorothy Day.* New York: Harper and Row, 1952.

Thea Bowman
Minister of Gospel Equality for All

Thea Bowman (1937–1990), a Franciscan Sister of Perpetual Adoration of La Crosse, Wisconsin, exemplified what it means to joyously celebrate the love of God while teaching the gospel of justice. An African American raised in Mississippi and a convert to Catholicism, Bowman courageously decided to join this Wisconsin religious community because the sisters embodied for her the embrace of Gospel equality for all persons. After a celebrated career in higher education, she turned her tremendous energy and love toward teaching others the beauty of a multicultural world. Bowman's love of music, her candid and uncompromising personal acceptance of all people, and her stirring reminders of the justice and peace implications of the Gospel made an impact on millions of people, from those on street corners to those worshiping in cathedrals. Even after being stricken with cancer in 1984, she traveled throughout the United States and to Africa, spreading the word of God.

MORNING

Call to Prayer

With the coming of each day, God offers the divine splendor of grace and spreads before us the human family arrayed in rich and wonderful diversity. The Creator invites us to celebrate in our diversity the fullness of God's life that binds us as one community. With Thea Bowman and all workers for equality, we are strengthened this day to confront the dark forces of discrimination and to open our arms wide to welcome others as Jesus does.

God of every race and nation,
in the beginning you fashioned our human nature
and stood over us with love
as the families of the world grew in your sight.
In Jesus you crowned for us the revelation of your will:
that you wish us to love one another
as you have loved us in Christ.
We confess our hardness of heart
and the pockets of fear and intolerance
for people unlike ourselves.
This day your Holy Spirit inspires us
to climb over the walls that divide us
and be bound as one people,
one family of love, proclaiming your glory.
Your love for us in Christ binds us in unity and love.

Praise

If we reflect together on the specific traditions which we embrace, our own ideas, values, and convictions are clarified, redefined and confirmed; our differences are understood; our commonalties are celebrated, and we are empowered for life in an ecumenical age and a pluralistic society. (Thea Bowman)

Reading

We celebrate the gift of our unity among the diversity of our human family. We are grateful for the power of the Spirit, who binds us in Christ as one people. In joy we pray: *Honor, love, and praise be yours!*

Acclamations

- We adore you, God, who has fashioned us as one people from many races and nations, as we pray . . .
- We are grateful for the gifts of all people that give glory to the multitude of graces that God holds out for all creation, as we pray . . .
- We honor you, God, whose loving Spirit breaks down the walls of hatred, prejudice, and discrimination, as we pray . . .
- We are filled with joy for the message of the Gospel that moves us to embrace all people as our sisters and brothers, as we pray . . .

Closing | God of all creation, you fashioned us in love. You bid us to love one another with the same passion with which Jesus poured out your presence in our midst. In the spirit of Thea Bowman, breathe forth your power of creation and break down the walls of hatred and discrimination. Bind us always in Christ as one people ever tending this world as the garden of your delights. Amen.

EVENING

Call to Prayer | Daylight is ending, and the night is coming. Yet we know that from dark corners of the human spirit, forces rob thousands of their security and dignity because they are judged as different. With Thea Bowman and all who work for justice and compassion, we ask God to kindle in our midst the lamp of Christ that strengthens us to work for justice and peace until the coming of the fullness of God's Reign.

Thanksgiving | O God, who rested from your labors on the seventh day,
you have given to our human family
the mission of tending the beauty and dignity of all
    creation.
You fashioned diverse peoples and races
to witness to the bright spectrum of your loving.
Into our world, you sent your only begotten Son
to speak forth the truth of your loving
that alone is our salvation.
Stretched out upon the cross,
Jesus gave his life for us
that we might learn to love one another
as you have loved us from the beginning.
In the rising of Christ,
you gave the greatest gift;
death has been conquered.
In this nighttime you stand by us faithfully,
teaching us in Christ to sacrifice for the good
and to hope for the promised glory,
especially for those the world has robbed
of their dignity as your daughters and sons,

your messengers of grace until the day of your coming. Your love alone binds us as your family.

[People often ask me how I keep going.] My early training is part of the ethic that enables me to do that. Old people in the black community taught us that we should serve the Lord until we die. We can even serve the Lord on our deathbeds or in any circumstances in life. If we have faith, hope and love we can pass it on. (Thea Bowman)

Reading

God has created us to live in harmony and love and to bind all people into the one family of grace. With Thea Bowman and all those who work for equal rights, we bring our needs before the God of all graces, as we pray: *Keep us mindful of your love.*

Intercessions

- For all Christians, that our efforts to build up the one Body of Christ may be a witness to all of the unity of the human family, let us pray . . .
- For all those who work for racial and human equality, that their hands may always be strengthened by the Holy Spirit, let us pray . . .
- For all those who oppress others because of human hatred, that the Spirit may lead them to break free from their bondage and sin, let us pray . . .
- For those who suffer at the hands of human hatred and bigotry, that our loving may be God's balm for their life, let us pray . . .

Repeat morning's closing.

Closing

More on Thea Bowman
Cepress, Celestine, ed. *Sister Thea Bowman: Shooting Star.* Winona, MN: Saint Mary's Press, 1993.

Acknowledgments *(continued)*

The scriptural passages in this book are freely adapted. These adaptations are not to be understood or used as official translations of the Bible.

The excerpt on page 44 by Augustine is from *Famous Conversations: The Christian Experience*, edited by Hugh T. Kerr and John M. Mulder (Grand Rapids, MI: William B. Eerdmans Publishing Company, 1983), pages 13–14. Copyright © 1983 by William B. Eerdmans Publishing Company.

The excerpt on pages 45–46 by Augustine is from *Augustine of Hippo: Selected Writings*, translated by Mary T. Clark (New York: Paulist Press, 1984), pages 125–126. Copyright © 1984 by Mary T. Clark.

The excerpts on pages 48 and 49 are adapted from "The Breastplate of Saint Patrick," as cited in *The Saint Book*, by Mary Reed Newland (San Francisco: Harper and Row, 1979), page 49. Copyright © 1979 by Seabury Press.

The excerpt on page 52 by Augustine is from *The Rule of Saint Augustine*, as cited in *The Day of Pentecost: Constitutions of the Canons Regular of Premontre* (DePere, WI: Saint Norbert Abbey, 1981), pages 16–17. Copyright © 1981 by Saint Norbert Abbey.

The prayer on pages 53–54 by Francis of Assisi is from *Francis and Clare: The Complete Works*, translation and introduction by Regis J. Armstrong, OFM Cap., and Ignatius C. Brady, OFM, preface by John Vaughn, OFM (Mahwah, NJ: Paulist Press, 1982), page 115. Copyright © 1982 by the Missionary Society of St. Paul the Apostle in the State of New York and the Society for Promoting Christian Knowledge.

The excerpt on page 56 by Hildegard of Bingen is from *"Scivias" by Hildegard of Bingen*, translated by Bruce Hozeski (Sante Fe, NM: Bear and Company, 1986), page 342. Copyright © 1986 by Bear and Company.

The excerpt on page 58 by Aelred of Rievaulx is from *On Spiritual Friendship*, translated by Mary Eugenia Laker, SSND (Washington, DC: Cistercian Publications, 1974), pages 72–73. Copyright © 1974 by Cistercian Publications. Used with permission.

The excerpt on page 61 by Anthony of Padua is adapted from *Seek First His Kingdom*, edited by Livio Poloniato, OFM Conv. (Padua, Italy: Prov. Pad. F.M.C. Editrice Grafiche Messaggero di S. Antonio, 1988), pages 133–134. Copyright © 1988 by Prov. Pad. F.M.C. Editrice Grafiche Messaggero di S. Antonio.

The prayer on page 62 by Anthony of Padua is from *Praise to You Lord: Prayers of Saint Anthony*, translated by Claude Jarmak (Padua, Italy: Prov. Pad. F.M.C. Editrice Grafiche Messaggero di S. Antonio, 1986), page 6. Copyright © 1986 Prov. Pad. F.M.C. Editrice Grafiche Messaggero di S. Antonio.

The excerpts on pages 125 and 126–127 by Sojourner Truth are quoted from *The Norton Anthology of Literature by Women*, by Sandra M. Gilbert and Susan Gubar (New York: W. W. Norton and Company, 1985), page 253. Copyright © 1985 by Sandra M. Gilbert and Susan Gubar. Used with permission.

The excerpts on pages 129 and 130–131 by Susan B. Anthony are from *Failure Is Impossible: Susan B. Anthony in Her Own Words,* by Lynn Sherr (New York: Random House, 1995), pages 297 and 249. Copyright © 1995 by Lynn Sherr. Used with permission.

The excerpts on pages 133 and 134 by Thérèse of Lisieux are from the *Autobiography of Saint Thérèse of Lisieux,* translated by Ronald Knox (New York: P. J. Kenedy and Sons, 1958), pages 237 and 289. Copyright © 1958 by P. J. Kenedy and Sons, copyright renewed. Used with permission.

The excerpts on pages 137 and 138–139 by Frances Xavier Cabrini are from *Immigrant Saint: The Life of Mother Cabrini*, by Pietro Di Donato (New York: McGraw-Hill Book Company, 1960), pages 90–91 and 184. Copyright © 1960 by Pietro Di Donato. Used by permission of the publisher.

The excerpt on page 141 is from *Alcoholics Anonymous* (New York: Alcoholics Anonymous World Services, 1976), page 63. Copyright © 1939, 1955, 1976 by Alcoholics Anonymous World Services.

The excerpt on pages 142–143 by Gerald May, MD, is from *Addiction and Grace* (New York: Harper and Row, 1988), pages 149–150. Copyright © 1988 by Gerald G. May.

The excerpt on page 145 by Pope John XXIII is from *The Encyclical Letter Pacem in Terris* (Washington, DC: National Catholic Welfare Conference, 1963), page 7. Copyright © 1963 by the Vatican Press Office.

The excerpt on page 146 is from the *Pastoral Constitution on the Church in the Modern World* (Washington, DC: National Catholic Welfare Conference, 1965), number 4. Copyright © 1965 by the National Catholic Welfare Conference.

The excerpt on page 149 by Thomas Merton is from *New Seeds of Contemplation* (New York: New Directions, 1962), pages 296–297. Copyright © 1961 by the Abbey of Gethsemani.

The excerpt on pages 150–151 by Thomas Merton is from *Conjectures of a Guilty Bystander* (Garden City, NY: Image Books, 1968), pages 80–81. Copyright © 1966 by the Abbey of Gethsemani.

The excerpt on page 153 by Dietrich Bonhoeffer is from *Christ the Center,* translated by Edwin H. Robertson (San Francisco: HarperSanFrancisco, 1965), page 11. Copyright © 1960 by Christian Kaiser Verlag; copyright © 1966 in the English translation by William Collins, Sons and Company, London; and Harper and Row, Publishers, New York.